The American Revolution, 1760–1790

In *The American Revolution, 1760–1790: New Nation as New Empire*, Neil L. York details the important and complex events that transpired during the creation of the enduring American Republic. This text presents a global look at the emerging nation's quest to balance liberty and authority before, during, and after the conflict with Great Britain, from the fall of Montreal through the Nootka Sound controversy. Through reviewing the causes and consequences of the Revolutionary era, York uncovers the period's paradoxes in an accessible, introductory text.

Taking an international perspective which closely examines the diplomatic and military elements of this period, this volume includes:

- Detailed maps of the Colonies, with important battle scenes highlighted
- Suggestions for further reading, allowing for more specialized research
- Comprehensive international context, providing background to Great Britain's relations with other European powers

Brief in length but broad in scope, York's text provides the ideal introductory volume to the Revolutionary War as well as the creation of American democracy.

Neil L. York is Professor of History at Brigham Young University, Provo, Utah.

The American Revolution, 1760–1790

New Nation as New Empire

Neil L. York

Routledge
Taylor & Francis Group

NEW YORK AND LONDON

First published 2016
by Routledge
711 Third Avenue, New York, NY 10017

and by Routledge
2 Park Square, Milton Park, Abingdon, Oxon, OX14 4RN

Routledge is an imprint of the Taylor & Francis Group, an informa business

British Library Cataloguing in Publication Data
A catalogue record for this book is available from the British Library

Library of Congress Cataloging in Publication Data
Names: York, Neil Longley, author.Title: The American Revolution, 1760-1790 : new nation as new empire / Neil York.Description: New York, NY : Routledge, 2016. | Includes index.Identifiers: LCCN 2015047676| ISBN 9781138838567 (hardback) | ISBN 9781138838574 (pbk.) | ISBN 9781315733791 (e-book)Subjects: LCSH: United States-- History--Revolution, 1775-1783. | United States--History--Confederation, 1783-1789. | United States--History--Colonial period, ca. 1600-1775. Classification: LCC E208 .Y669 2016 | DDC 973.3--dc23LC record available at http://lccn.loc.gov/2015047676

ISBN: 978-1-138-83856-7 (hbk)
ISBN: 978-1-138-83857-4 (pbk)
ISBN: 978-1-315-73379-1 (ebk)

Typeset in Sabon by
Servis Filmsetting Ltd, Stockport, Cheshire

Printed and bound in the United States of America by Publishers Graphics, LLC on sustainably sourced paper.

To
Jen and Cait
no father ever had finer daughters
and to
Carole
their devoted mother; my loving wife

Contents

PART II
World War

PART III
Nation as Empire

Acknowledgments

I first started thinking about writing a book like this a dozen years ago. By then I had been teaching a course on Revolutionary America for over twenty years and had used a half-dozen different texts over that time. At the same dinner table with Jack Greene, Peter Onuf, and Christopher Brown—distinguished historians all—I could not resist asking them what books they required in their own courses. Martin Flaherty, a law professor, was there too and he weighed in on the conversation. Thoughts that I had thereafter about doing a text of my own lay dormant for a decade, when Kim Guinta invited me to try my hand at it. I had already worked with Kim on a Boston Massacre book for Routledge and jumped at the chance. Since then, Genevieve Aoki, Margo Irvin, and Dan Finaldi at Routledge have made each step on the path to publication a pleasure. Anna Dolan skillfully oversaw production; Janice Baiton handled the copyediting; and Bookbright Media provided the index. Colleague Chris Hodson recommended that I ask Alice Thiede to do the maps. I did, she consented, and the excellent results speak for themselves.

Jack Greene, long retired from teaching at Johns Hopkins but still a very active scholar, was kind enough to read the entire manuscript. He offered very helpful suggestions, as did Colin Nicolson of the University of Stirling. Routledge solicited reviews from three anonymous readers and their suggestions too improved what you now have in hand. In fact, this book took the form it did because of the many scholars whose works on Revolutionary America I have read over the past four decades, and the students who have taken courses from me over that same span. All of them have played a part in shaping my view of the past, and how to teach it.

Preface

There are a fair number of textbooks in print that survey Revolutionary American history, so readers may wonder why I have added yet another to that list. It is a given that no book can cover everything. I, like all authors, decided what I wanted to emphasize, which meant leaving out some themes discussed by other historians and including themes that they passed over. Like them, I have chosen what I consider to be effective starting and ending points, and my narrative of the events in between is no more or less interpretive than theirs. That is the nature of historical writing, whatever the form it may take or whoever the intended audience may be.

This book is a "brief" or "short" history of the American Revolution only in the most literal sense. That is to say, it is not very long. I have not attempted to say a little about this and a little about that in a futile attempt to mention everything worth mentioning. Rather, I concentrated on certain topics that I think best represent the dynamics defining the Revolutionary Era. Those I examined in some depth.

What I see as the most important element in the emergence of Revolutionary America is the quest to balance liberty and authority within the framework of an expansive, dynamic society—a forward-looking nation that also tried to keep certain ties to the past. At the core of political principles espoused in Britain and its American colonies was a constitutionalist's notion of fundamental law. What is most intriguing is how leaders of the Revolutionary generation attempted to secure their rights, even as their desire to extend their trade, enlarge their territory, preserve their political domination, and fulfill a profound sense of destiny complicated their efforts.

I have been nibbling around the edges of that larger concern for quite some time now, in various books and articles. Thus I have written about Ireland's disputes with Britain, disputes that paralleled those of the American colonies. I have also explored the colonists' unmet demands for rights within the empire, the numerous proposals for reform suggested on both sides of the Atlantic, and, ultimately, the Revolutionary American assumption that what Britons had done with their empire they could do better in their own nation. Before turning to those topics, I had examined foreign aid to the revolutionaries and the fighting on American battlefields. This text is the culmination of all those earlier studies, combined with what I have gathered over the years to teach my Revolutionary America course.

My choice of 1760 as the opening year and 1790 as the closing offers some indication of the choices that I made in framing what follows. In 1760, Montreal fell to a combined force of British regulars, colonial militia, and Indian allies. New France would not formally become part of the British empire for another three years but astute observers at the time knew that the long Anglo-French struggle for domination of North America would end in Britain's favor. A few anticipated a new conflict that would pit Britain against its own colonies, victory over France, ironically, providing the impetus for that conflict.

Just as 1760 and the fall of Montreal seemed a good starting point, the Nootka Sound controversy of 1790 struck me as a good place to end. That same year Rhode Island ratified a new constitution that had come out of the Philadelphia convention well over two years before, a constitution under which the nation had been governed for just over a year. With ratification completed in all thirteen states, the new political order had a legitimacy and stability it had lacked until that moment, which improved its standing in the broader world. That in turn enabled the new nation of states to make its presence felt beyond its borders, even to the Pacific coast reaches of Nootka Sound, in a way that those states as colonies in the old empire could not have done.

The expanded British empire that had resulted from the fall of New France did not last long before being shaken to its core. The reconfigured American nation marked by full ratification of the Constitution would also eventually be shaken, though after a much longer period of time and with a decidedly different outcome. In that prior conflict, the Americans who chose to leave the British empire succeeded in founding their own nation. In the second, a later generation of Americans would attempt to secede and reconstitute themselves as the Confederate States of America. They failed in their quest but differences were reconciled and a united nation was restored. On some fundamental level, then, the issues that had divided Britons from Americans and led to revolution in 1776 had run deeper than the issues that set Americans against each other in 1861.

Any review of the causes and consequences of the American Revolution entails accepting the role played by contingency and the ironic, even paradoxical, nature of developments over those years. There are certain basics that readers should keep in mind as they peruse the story I have chosen to tell here. First and foremost is to recognize that the Revolutionary movement occurred on a larger world stage. There is no clear causal dividing line between developments in the British colonies of North America and developments in the rest of the empire. Change was the one constant everywhere, though that change was not obvious to many and resisted by some.

For colonists to think of themselves as British Americans was the natural order of things, which is why the empire was idealized as a family, with Britain as the mother country and the colonies as the children, or at the very least promoted as a community of the like-minded with shared interests. These were not mere rhetorical devices; they were expressions of deeply held beliefs not easily abandoned, on either side of the Atlantic.

Consequently, the vast majority of Americans who eventually founded an independent nation began as reluctant revolutionaries. Those who were students of Greek and Roman history understood that nations crumble and empires fall, and yet they initially sought to secure their rights within the British empire rather than strike off on their own. Stereotype notwithstanding, Samuel Adams and most other future American revolutionaries spent more time trying to reconcile differences within the empire than looking for excuses to leave it. Likewise, policy makers in London charged with running the empire were not, as stereotype would have it, fey villains or witless fools. Foreseeing disaster from a growing dispute over the extent of colonial liberty and limit to imperial authority, there were those in Britain who urged that Americans be seated in their parliament or be encouraged to create an inter-colonial legislature or even be allowed legislative autonomy through their individual colonies. Ultimately, the reformers calling for change did not prevail, but not because those who opposed them were blind to the problems that existed.

There was never a time when the fighting that finally erupted in 1775 was contained within the empire's bounds. The Americans' alliance with the French in 1778 did not mark some sort of fundamental change, from civil war to international conflict. The dispute had always been transatlantic, even worldwide, in scope. Indeed, protesting colonists were emboldened to take up arms as rebels because they anticipated help from abroad and hoped to turn European balance of power struggles to their advantage.

True enough, the British did not apply force effectively to restore imperial authority in the rebellious colonies and they sought to negotiate as well as coerce, from beginning to end. The military outcome was determined as much by political events over the horizon as on American soil, with British leaders repeatedly debating what they could do to save their empire. Moreover, important as the actions of American diplomats were in securing treaties with France and a generous peace from Britain, there was much done in the diplomatic give and take that was simply beyond their control. To characterize the war as primarily an American victory achieved with only some foreign assistance, as if events in the colonies can be separated from events abroad, is to misconstrue the underlying dynamic in the controversies leading to war, not just the war itself.

Readers ought to consider this as well: leaving the British empire did not *ipso facto* solve the basic American problem of building a more satisfying political order. Revolutionary Americans had demanded and failed to receive what they deemed a sufficient share of power within the British empire. The informal federalism that some had fought for within that empire was pursued more formally in the new nation. Although political independence gave Americans the opportunity to experiment with republicanism in their own unique federal arrangement, questions about ultimate sovereignty, so troubling within the empire, remained problematical in the new nation. The national government had to deal with subordinate territories and what it deemed to be subject peoples as well as work out its relationship with the states. In so doing it confronted problems echoing those earlier faced by crown and parliament in the old empire. Even so, those who led the new nation wanted to believe that it could be an empire built without the taint of imperialism. Confident as they may have been that they had a brighter future ahead once they were freed from Britain, they were also dogged by doubts and haunted by fears that their experiment could fail—that they, like others before them, would not bring about Virgil's ideal of a "new order of the ages."

Prologue

British regulars and local militiamen shed each other's blood in the Massachusetts countryside on April 19, 1775. Something had gone dreadfully wrong: Americans fighting Britons in what was supposed to be a shared transatlantic community, a community that some even characterized as a family. Twenty years before that confrontation, John Adams had contemplated a future where Americans could choose their own destiny, though an Anglo-American war had not been part of his vision. Waxing philosophical, he observed that change is inevitable, that "even mighty States and kingdoms" that rise to sway the fortunes of the globe eventually fall. Then aged nineteen and just completing his studies at Harvard College, Adams had been raised in Braintree, a close-knit farming community. A half-day's horse ride south of Boston, Braintree was a tiny part of Massachusetts, itself but one small colony in Great Britain's flourishing American enterprise—which was, in turn, contained within an even more expansive overseas empire. To Adams, Britain stood as the world's colossus, as Rome once had before. Perhaps, Adams, speculated, within a century the "great seat of empire" would be transferred to his side of the Atlantic and British Americans could lead the way to new cultural heights. To do this they must first remove the "turbulent Gallicks" to the north; after that, nothing would stand in their way.

Adams did not write as a future American revolutionary, at least not consciously. As a young man on the make, he would soon put aside teaching and turn to law, seeing the courtroom rather than the school house as a more likely place to realize his ambitions. It is not clear what prompted him to pick that moment for pondering what lay ahead for his homeland. Perhaps he had heard of the fighting that erupted a few months before on the Pennsylvania frontier, pitting British regulars and American militiamen against the French and their Indian allies in what would unfold as the great contest over continental domination. Perhaps, too, he had read Benjamin Franklin's recently published *Observations*, which suggested that American growth would be so rapid that the colonial population would surpass that of the mother country over the next one hundred years. With wealth generated in fertile soil worked by industrious settlers, Franklin predicted, the British-American frontier would become irresistible as a land of opportunity for those in the Old World seeking a better life in the New.

Eventually Franklin and Adams were brought together by their shared American dream, though they began as defenders of American rights in the British empire before they became champions of an independent American nation. As with so many others in the Revolutionary generation, politics would make strange bedfellows. Franklin and Adams were separated by thirty years in age and homes three hundred miles apart. Their personalities were striking in their differences: Franklin the amiable cosmopolite, Adams the acerbic yankee. Those differences notwithstanding, together they declared independence; together they sought foreign aid to sustain their cause; together they helped negotiate the peace that secured their new nation. And yet theirs was always an awkward, sometimes strained, relationship and the difficulty of their working together was a microcosm of the difficulties of nation-building, of somehow, as Adams put it, getting thirteen clocks to strike as one. More often than not there was a cacophony of sounds, not a harmonious chiming; reconciling very real differences with vague notions of a united nation proved daunting.

As the noted historian Gordon Wood observed, leaders of the Revolutionary generation were only half aware of where their actions would take them. They, like people everywhere, would learn to live with the law of unintended consequences. Benjamin Franklin could not have known that his political preferences would eventually cause a rift between himself and his son, William. Once close, they never reconciled in what was in fact our first true civil war. John Adams and his oldest son, John Quincy—both future presidents—had the opposite experience. The younger Adams accompanied his father to Europe and, as a teenager, witnessed his father's attempts to protect American interests abroad. Like his father, John Quincy would later wonder if their new nation had chosen the right course—not so much in its relations to the outside world, but by the choices it was making within its own borders. Both the Adamses and the Franklins experienced first-hand the dual tendencies of nation-building: agreement and disagreement, clarity and confusion, construction and destruction, union and dis-union. Those dynamics had been at play since the beginning of colonization. They continue even now.

Part I

Empire as Nation

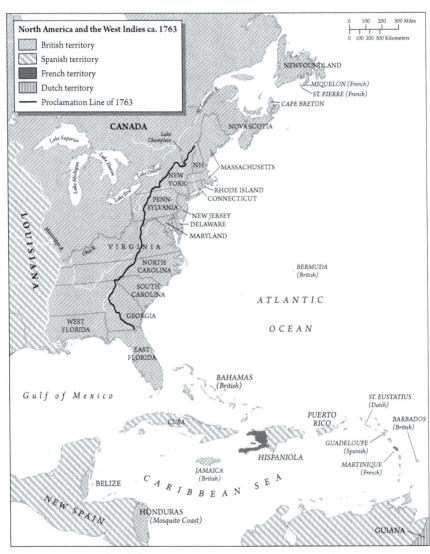

Map 1 North America and the West Indies ca. 1763. Map by Alice Thiede, CARTO-GRAPHICS

Chapter 1

Imperial Dreams, Colonial Realities

Britain Triumphant

Montreal fell to the British in September 1760 and with it went France's empire in North America. Its surrender had been predicted by those closest to the fighting but the event itself had actually been a near thing. Less than six months before the French had launched a campaign to retake Quebec, which had been surrendered to the British the previous year. A British fleet with reinforcements made it to Quebec just in time; British naval superiority prevented the French from doing the same. The French retreated back toward Montreal to await what now appeared to have become inevitable.

An Anglo-American land and naval force of well over fifteen thousand, advancing in three columns, converged on the city; it would be given up without much of a fight. The French had been outnumbered at better than three to one, with no hope of relief. Anticipating defeat and not relishing being caught in a siege, New France's Indian allies drifted away as the British came closer. Some may have switched sides to join the natives already allied with the British. Even the local militia proved reluctant to muster forth and defend Montreal to the last. Major General Jeffrey Amherst had mounted a well-coordinated campaign, as British regulars, colonial American militia, and Indian warriors combined their efforts. Even though they did not mesh together perfectly as some sort of well-oiled military machine, gone were the earlier days of humiliation, marked especially by General Edward Braddock's defeat in 1755. Then, British regulars had been slaughtered by an unseen enemy in the Pennsylvania woods. What happened to Braddock proved to be an anomaly; British regulars were crucial to the eventual Anglo-American victory. Red regimental coats or tartan kilts did not have to be cast aside in order to fight successfully in North America.

As so often happens in the ironies of life, the satisfying short-term outcome also had its less satisfying long-term effect. We can now see that victory sowed with it the seeds of defeat. What is hindsight for us was foresight for others. That there was a potentially dangerous dynamic at work in the British empire had been noticed by two men thousands of miles away from Montreal. One was English, the other French; neither would ever set foot on American soil. Both were in Constantinople, friends despite being on different sides in this most recent war. The Frenchman commented—his ironic intent transparent—that France ought to be heartened and the British chastened. With the French driven out of North America, Britons and Americans would find themselves turning on each other, one-time allies becoming enemies. Why? Because Americans would be called on by Britons to help share the greater financial burdens brought by a larger empire. But they, the Frenchman predicted, "will answer you by shaking off all dependence." The Englishman, John Lind, would, during that future conflict, write in defense of Britain's imperial policy and against the American response to it. The Frenchman, Charles Gravier, Comte de Vergennes, as France's wartime foreign minister would be in a position to turn his prediction into a self-fulfilling prophecy.

The Anglo-French struggle for overseas empire that took Amherst's juggernaut to the gates of Montreal had begun roughly seventy years before. Competition between England and France for empire closer to home dated back centuries rather than decades, long before either nation looked toward the Atlantic horizon. The Great Britain that would come to define itself by overseas empire had once been an England with far more modest ambitions, as it attempted to secure its place in the home islands and hold on to tenuous claims in France. English interest in overseas empire did not lead immediately to the New World. Likewise, English interest in New World commercial wealth did not lead immediately to the planting of colonies there. And for much of colonial American history, what had been settled on the mainland mattered less to Britain's imperially minded than what had developed in the West Indies.

Imperial England

For those on the island of Great Britain who preferred tribal living and local control, the creation of England itself was a type of imperialism. England's Angevin empire, an eventual by-product of the Norman invasion in the eleventh century, was more self-consciously ambitious than empires that had gone before. But the Anglo-Saxons who resented those Normans—as they had resented the Danes who invaded just a generation before—had earlier subjugated ancient Britons. Those ancient Britons no doubt resented them, as those Britons had resented the Romans who beat them into submission centuries earlier. England, then, long before it became Great Britain with the Scottish parliamentary union in 1707, had been formed by a concentration of authority and power—celebrated by some, denigrated by others.

With good reason did historian Hugh Kearney advise us to take a "Britannic approach" to studying the land and people of those isles, at least into the sixteenth century. Thinking only within the boundaries that would someday mark England, Scotland, Wales, and Ireland eliminates important nuances. Differences that divided people under the same rulers or cultural connections that transcended feudal borders can be lost if studies begin with the nation state in embryo. Kearney noted that there is a tendency to "domesticate the Norman Conquest" of 1066, as if there was something foreordained about what followed, a playing out of a time-honored tale that takes us sequentially from Saxon England to Norman England to the England of the Tudors and then the England that gave us Virginia.

To think of the emergence of England as a product of conquest and colonization *within* the British Isles can better help us understand the forces at work when England moved *beyond* those island realms, and beyond a France that English kings, beginning with Edward III in the fourteenth century, claimed as rightfully theirs. Historians have long commented that the notions of cultural, even racial, superiority that Anglo-Normans, and later the English, took with them to Celtic Ireland, settlers carried across the Atlantic as well. Native Americans would suffer the consequences. But with Kearney's caution in mind, we should also remember that those attitudes had been part of England's dealings with Wales and Scotland as well as Ireland—even as England itself was developing its own identity. Attachment to an idealized England composed of a single, homogenous people was an ideological construct. It was necessary for the development of what French sociologist Émile Durkheim called the "collective consciousness" behind national identity, but a construct nonetheless. England was born in a belief system that acted as the foundation for an eventual worldwide empire that needed to think of itself as an organic community of interests, even a family of mother country and children colonies: English nation as precursor to British empire. But within that British empire the English would maintain a self-conscious cultural core. The sense of manifest destiny and mission that would someday drive Americans to strike out on their own was a direct outgrowth of England's earlier expansion that had joined nation and empire. Likewise for the American identity behind it, which retained much about it that was English.

Overseas Empire

"Commerce follows the flag" proclaimed Senator Henry Cabot Lodge in his 1895 defense of American expansionism. He advocated a vigorous American foreign policy in neighboring lands—neighboring lands that extended to Hawaii as an essential "outwork" of the American "citadel." Critics of Lodge's jingoism would point out that, more often than not, the flag actually follows commerce—the national public interest abroad being defined by the trail carved or wake cut by private enterprise that ventured forth first. British imperial historian P. J. Marshall offered a variation on that distinction when he differentiated between British "expansion" and the British "empire." The private enterprise of the former tended to precede the public policy of the latter and define the priorities set by those charged with imperial administration. Expansion existed apart from empire and yet they were "closely linked and mutually dependent," as Professor Marshall put it. The movement of Americans beyond their borders once they achieved political independence mimicked the tendencies of Britons begun nearly two centuries before: exploration of new worlds, the out-migration of settlers, uneasy relations often leading to clashes between indigenous peoples and transplanted Europeans, the development of trade ties between homeland and new colonies, subsequent economic and social transformations, the building of political communities, and the intellectual apparatus that would underpin it all, but much of it rather loose knit if not haphazard as it unfolded.

Reconceptualizing the ocean as a barrier into the ocean as a highway may have been the most fundamental discovery of the so-called Age of Discovery. England became an essential part of this reconfiguration, as were Portugal, Spain, and the Netherlands before it, and France at roughly the same time. They pioneered what later scholars would call the world economic system, which became the foundation of our modern interconnected lives. Tentative transoceanic travel evolved into a constant flow of peoples, goods, and ideas around the globe.

The nation state as it emerged in western Europe stood at the core of this enterprise. Creating worldwide markets boosted capitalist enterprise, with the accumulation of wealth and concentration of power. Setting up trading outposts in one part of the world and encouraging the growth of settler colonies in another transformed the nations that led the way and the native societies drawn into their orbits. Questions of national identity and state sovereignty, already complicated, became even more complex with the drawing together of peoples and cultures that had once existed in relative isolation from each other. Even though the Atlantic world of 1776 was essentially pre-industrial, there had been a proliferation of goods and growth of consumer culture that gave an increasingly materialistic tinge to what constituted the good life, and the expectations of those living in colonies who nonetheless expected to share its blessings.

When John Cabot set forth from England in 1497 so that the island nation could claim a share of whatever it was Columbus had found to the west in a search for the East, he sailed into an Atlantic that Spain and Portugal had already divided between them. They did so with papal sanction, the Vatican continuing its century-old practice of mediating disputes between rival European states over Atlantic islands. The most sweeping of those papal decrees came in 1493, in direct response to Columbus's first voyage. The Spanish and Portuguese followed it the next year with the now famous Treaty of Tordesillas. Bisecting the Atlantic, all pagan lands to the west of the line were left open to Spain; those to the south and east were deemed within Portugal's sphere. Any other Christian nation venturing into those climes did so as an interloper, interfering with the building of God's kingdom on Earth.

Portugal and Spain began a shift in wealth and power in Europe, as the trade domination of Italian city states in the Mediterranean and the Hanse in the Baltic would be eclipsed by Atlantic enterprise. Portugal had extended its reach as far as the Azores by the 1440s and to various island groups off Africa as well as to the coast of Africa itself. Spain came close on its heels; England lagged far behind. All would mix public policy with private enterprise because none of these nation states had the wherewithal to pursue transoceanic empire. They had to expand on the cheap, which meant they had had no choice but to build a potential conflict of interests into their overseas efforts. Threats to their security or stability would eventually come from disagreements within as well as rivals without.

Spain would unsuccessfully attempt to use its papally endorsed treaties with Portugal to keep competitors like England out of its New World enterprises. The presumed right of discovery that lay at the heart of the Spanish enterprise would be adopted and then modified by the English. Potential confrontation between these rivals did not automatically produce open conflict. Spain realized, as the decades passed, that it could not make good on all of its New World claims. It finally grudgingly accepted the reality of English America when, in 1670, it recognized the legitimacy of the Carolina colony to the north of St. Augustine. Still, it did not accept Carolina's western and southern boundary claims. Spain had over twenty years before it recognized Dutch independence and, with it, the right of the Dutch to trade in areas of the world that, according to Spain's 1494 arrangement with Portugal, was forbidden. In abandoning the fiction of that monopoly, Spain accepted changes in both the Old World and the New that it could not prevent. The demands of "realpolitik," it learned, could only be resisted for so long. Like the French and the English as well as the Dutch, the Spanish adjusted their diplomatic and military responses to the needs of the moment.

The long dreamt-of China trade that had prompted Spain to back Columbus also proved alluring to the English. Those wanting to develop the western route overseas vied with those interested in pressing east through the interior of Asia. The Muscovy Company concentrated on exploring the far north to find a great river that could take merchants deep inland, perhaps to China itself. The Levant Company concentrated on the eastern Mediterranean as the starting point for its overland trade to the east. Although it did not prosper, some of its investors shifted their emphasis to the newly founded East India Company in 1600, which for nearly three centuries would be the face of Britain's empire on the Indian subcontinent. The motto "Deus Indicat" inscribed on the East India Company's coat of arms captured the sentiments of these enterprises and others coming after: that God led them in their efforts, that England's empire was somehow also His, its success a reflection of His will. All of these joint stock companies were founded after England's early enthusiasm for New World adventure had waned. That enthusiasm was preserved on a small scale among the "Sea Dogs" like John Hawkins and Francis Drake—and of course those who had long been fishing for cod off the Grand Banks but who showed little interest in colony-planting schemes.

Once the English did develop a sustained interest in the New World, the most far-sighted among them envisioned a European balance of power remade because of it. Henry VII had expected Cabot to avoid direct confrontation with the Spanish over territorial claims. So were his successors for generations to come, until the migratory trickle became an irresistible flood. Richard Hakluyt captured England's transatlantic imperial vision perfectly in his 1584 "Discourse" on western planting. A tract seen only by a few in Hakluyt's lifetime, it nevertheless captured the ambitions of that generation, ambitions that would be recognizable even centuries later. Hakluyt's ideas were to be absorbed within a historical understanding that embraced the notion of American exceptionalism—that here was a unique land of opportunity awaiting a dynamic people to exploit it. Reviewing tales of pre-Columbian voyages to America by Britons, Hakluyt emphasized effective occupation over prior discovery when it came to claiming rights over new lands and peoples. That view defined the approach England took over the centuries as it transformed itself and the native peoples it drew within its global sphere. Americans would someday echo it when they had an expansive nation of their own.

Hakluyt, an Anglican priest, talked of a religious transformation. Pagans in the New World would be brought to God through English colonization and the religiously oppressed in Europe would have a new haven. Since Hakluyt lived in post-Reformation England, he had in mind an Anglican, not a Catholic, God at the center of English-American life. That Hakluyt may have been culturally blind, his idea of liberation striking many indigenous peoples as subjugation, did not make him insincere.

Hakluyt emphasized that England's poor could make a new start in that New World. They would plant the crops, raise the livestock, and transfer the industries enabling England, through its overseas empire, to become more self-sufficient. Ideally it would develop a virtually self-contained economy with no need to trade outside its own transoceanic nexus. Even the Spanish—ahead of them in the overseas game at the moment—would someday turn to them for desirable goods. Moreover, the English-American producer would also be a consumer, helping to stimulate the economy back home. Indeed, England could convert transatlantic trade domination into

European political power, using the marketplace as a profitable and yet bloodless scene of competition.

In Hakluyt's trickle-down theory of imperial prosperity, all who were part of the enterprise would benefit. It is no surprise, then, that colonial Americans became attached to the idea of the good life, a hope that hard work would bring comfort and security, even wealth and status. With time they would gauge the success of the larger empire by how well it helped them realize their own dreams of prosperity.

Hakluyt anticipated a robust shipbuilding industry in English America and he was convinced that crossings there and back would be safer, speedier, and more reliable than the longer voyages to India and the Far East. England could free itself of a growing dependence on the Baltic states and ease pressures on its own shrinking raw materials for a blue water navy: oak for hulls and decks; pine for masts and spars; pitch, tar, and hemp for caulking and rigging. Hakluyt saw a future where the small vessels of his era would be replaced by massive merchantmen. Their holds would carry the wealth of empire and their decks would mount cannons to defend it. Hakluyt can be forgiven for not foreseeing the coming specialization in naval architecture, with a privately owned merchant marine that would be protected by a Royal Navy that carried guns, not goods. He did foresee that, with all of the private wealth indirectly benefiting the English crown by enriching the nation, there would also be a need to fill public coffers by taxing trade—not just articles carried by European rivals, but goods carried by the English and their American colonists. Cabot had only been expected to share with the Crown a percentage of the gold, silver and other precious metals he brought out of the New World. By Hakluyt's day all goods produced in the overseas empire could in theory be taxed, though Hakluyt and his contemporaries were far from working out the details of what would become known as the navigation system.

England's champions of overseas empire were all mercantilists who emphasized subordinating private enrichment to public security. According to this theory, bullion should flow into, not out of, the empire, as part of a favorable balance of trade where exports exceeded imports. But attachment to mercantilistic notions did not bring with it a prescribed set of policies. Any limitation on the flow of trade to constrain wealth was bound to provoke opposition, as the crown, privy council and parliament attempted to balance rival commercial interests within the empire. Placating producers could be as difficult as satisfying consumers. Attempts to monopolize trade brought automatic resistance and smuggling became a transoceanic way of life, proof that imperial ideal and colonial reality could be at odds. Ultimately, disputes over trade policies could lead to disputes over political rights.

Not all parts of the empire were equal. London responded more readily to the needs of some overseas enterprises than others. The expectations of

American colonists had to be weighed against the needs of others. Sometimes the resulting trade policies worked to their advantage; sometimes they did not. Many of the issues associated with the trade policies leading to the Boston Tea Party in December 1773 had been anticipated a century and a half before. Then the commodity concerned was tobacco rather than tea. Tobacco growers in Virginia wanted open access to markets and resented having to ship their leaf to England first before being able to sell on the continent. They also wanted a monopoly that would keep English planters from growing their own crop and Dutch or Spanish vessels from delivering tobacco originating elsewhere. London was only willing to go so far to accommodate them. Ironically, by the Revolutionary Era tobacco prices had dropped as the market became glutted, a problem caused more by over-planting than restrictive trade regulations. And yet as disgruntled Virginians saw it, London was somehow to blame.

To Virginians who might have contended that their economic stability depended on tobacco as much as the East India Company did on tea to stay solvent, imperial officials could have countered that the analogy was strained. Virginia was incorporated within the empire; India was essentially a foreign land and company officials constantly cultivated diplomatic ties to Indian rulers. They had almost no control over India's internal economy. Virginia was but a portion of British North America; the East India Company dealt with the entire Indian sub-continent. At the time of the Tea Act in 1773, so resented by American colonists because parliament used its authority to strengthen the East India Company's monopoly, the company was attempting to expand its presence in Bengal and consolidate recent gains in Madras. The stakes, simply put, were much higher there than in Virginia. Policies propping up the East India Company, despite its inefficient, even corrupt management, reflected that different priority.

Perennial transatlantic disagreements over priorities notwithstanding, English America eventually flourished after initial false starts. The colonial American economy on the eve of the Revolution was diverse and dynamic—notable attributes in this pre-industrial world. Generally speaking, the West Indies stood apart from the mainland in their emphasis on slave-labor plantations producing sugar and molasses from fields of cane. Even if a larger island like Jamaica—four times the size of Rhode Island, with a population nearly five times as large—did not literally depend on the mainland colonies to feed itself, commercial connections between them were strong. Jamaicans too resented attempts by London to curtail trade or limit local political autonomy.

The mainland had regional commercial economies, from the coastal rice and inland indigo grown in Georgia and South Carolina to the naval stores produced in North Carolina. Virginia and Maryland continued to grow tobacco, though wheat was becoming more common as it spread down from Pennsylvania and Delaware. New Jersey and New York produced foodstuffs for export, from beef to flour. New England's trees were harvested for lumber and its ships dominated the cod fisheries. Most colonists lived on the land and whatever wealth they generated came largely from their crops and livestock. At the same time, there were thriving merchant communities along the coast, from Georgia to New Hampshire.

Economic growth rates matched, even exceeded, those of England. Colonists not shackled in slavery tended to be better fed, clothed and housed than their cousins across the Atlantic. Overall their standard of living was probably higher, even as their taxes were considerably lower. The greater their self-sufficiency, the greater their desire for self-government. The population on the mainland far exceeded that in the West Indies, though the islands, even into the early 1770s, accounted for more of the wealth flowing into Britain through their sugar-based exports. By then the mainland North American colonies had a population of perhaps three million, the West Indies collectively less than a quarter of that—and fewer than sixty thousand of that total were free whites. It was not until the 1760s that residents on the mainland purchased more goods from the mother country than did people in the British Caribbean. If West Indians were better able to lobby for imperial policies that benefited them than those on the mainland, there was a good financial reason for it.

Nevertheless, the mainland American colonies and West Indies taken together accounted for only half of the goods flowing into and out of Britain. They lagged behind the Baltic, Mediterranean, and East Indian trade. Both were consequently limited in how much they could influence imperial policy. All too often what they considered anti-colonial was, from London's perspective, simply pro-empire. The goal of reciprocity, where all profited from being part of a larger enterprise, could be difficult to reach. Policies that pleased one set of interests could offend another. The idealized concept of an imperial greater good was difficult to sustain and the choice of rewarding one group through trade privileges or investment incentives while denying either to others vexed even the most skillful imperial officials. As with the adverse American reaction to the Iron Act of 1750, resentment was not necessarily because of what was being denied to the colonists at that moment. Rather, restrictions on economic enterprise—in the case of the Iron Act, on the fabrication of iron goods for export or the making of steel at all—caused colonists to fear what imperial policy portended for the future.

Administrative Anxieties

The distinguished historian Charles M. Andrews famously observed that Britain's imperial policy was always playing catch-up with colonial development. Ad hoc in implementation even if theoretically consistent over time, it was in constant flux. The crown and the privy council had attempted to direct international trade and control domestic enterprise associated with it almost from the beginning, but the administrative apparatus took shape very slowly. In 1651 parliament passed the first of the trade-regulating acts that marked the emergence of a navigation system that would still be in place in 1776. Foreign carriers were largely barred from trade in the empire; an increasing number of enumerated goods specifying what could go where had duties attached to them; some economic pursuits were encouraged with bounties and premiums while others were discouraged or forbidden altogether. Regulation and revenue-raising went hand in hand because London worried as much about one as the other.

All colonial charters were issued in the name of the crown; all legislation pertaining to the colonies went through crown and parliament. Fairly early on the crown and parliament had experts to advise them on policy making, the Board of Trade being the longest lived and most influential. An American secretary of state was added to the imperial bureaucracy in 1768. He joined the secretaries of state for the northern and southern departments, which had been in existence for over a century and a half before. The American secretary handled official correspondence between London and the individual colonies and, like Board of Trade members, made policy recommendations. He had responsibility for all of Britain's American holdings, not just the North American mainland. The creation of this office had as much to do with crown and parliamentary politics as the desire for greater administrative efficiency. But then running the empire would always have its political as well as its governmental side.

The colonists proved adept evaders of trade laws and smuggling ran rampant. Suggesting that worse was to come: the greater the effort to curtail illicit trade, the more it increased. Colonists claimed that those attempts violated their fundamental rights. Imperial officials countered that they misunderstood their place in the empire and the need for all to sacrifice for the greater good. Those differing perspectives explain John Hancock's dualistic image: notorious smuggler in the eyes of some imperial authorities in London; respected merchant among many fellow Bostonians. Juries in colonial common-law courts could not be relied upon to convict locals of trade act violations. As early as the 1670s, customs inspectors and vice-admiralty courts, where royally appointed judges ruled without juries, had been put in place to alter colonial smuggling habits. They most likely had the opposite effect. The more efficiently they did their jobs in detecting, prosecuting, and convicting smugglers, the more they were resented in the Catch-22 impossibilities that would come to typify imperial and colonial relations.

Adam Smith's condemnation of the "mercantile system" that gave form to these relationships came after Americans had revolted and were on the verge of declaring independence. The British empire may have "bred and formed the men" who succeeded in founding the American colonies, Smith conceded, but what had been achieved since that point they had done themselves. He contended that attempts by imperial authorities to limit their economic enterprise through trade laws were counterproductive and ultimately doomed to fail. Those laws were too concerned with a narrow notion of a favorable trade balance. They privileged a handful of producers in the mother country at the expense of consumers there and in the colonies, and they foreclosed opportunities for new producers to emerge in the colonies.

Smith, incidentally, repeated the warnings already coming from Josiah Tucker, who spilled considerably more ink on the colonies and their poor fit in mercantilistic policies than did Smith. Abrupt, direct, Tucker told the masters of empire they had five choices when it came to solving the American problem: they could do nothing; they could offer Americans seats in parliament; they could consider making an American city like New York or Philadelphia the new seat of empire; they could use force to drive Americans back into line; or they could let the Americans go altogether. His preference was for the last—not because he was a doctrinaire free trade enthusiast, but because he thought that Britain could dominate the American economy even with Americans outside the empire. Britain, he insisted, could enjoy all of the profits of trade with none of the headaches of administration.

Tucker echoed, more acerbically, earlier political economists who had advised that, for an expansive empire to survive over time, reciprocity had to be quantifiable, not simply rhetorical. Ultimately, talk of an imperial community of interests or a transatlantic Anglo-American family had to be matched by real conditions in order to be sustained. But as Smith as well as Tucker pointed out, all too often discord overshadowed harmony. Only with the American war that erupted in 1775 would some British policy makers come around to Tucker's or Smith's way of thinking.

Failed Experiment

Originally English America, the Virginia of the 1580s, had no precise boundaries. Clearer boundaries came over time, as the once vague Virginia was subdivided into more and more distinct colonies. One of the new claimants within the original but now re-configured Virginia was the Massachusetts Bay Company, which received a crown charter in 1629. In less than a decade, Charles I wanted to revoke the charter he had granted. Sabers rattled as imperial authorities prepared to impose their authority in the Bay Colony and the settlers there prepared to resist. Although the crisis passed, the underlying causes for it remained—indeed, were never wholly eliminated. In essence, Massachusetts wanted a political autonomy that its king would not allow. The charter from Charles I that it lost, parliament restored during the civil war of the 1640s. Even so, the Bay Colony sought a degree of independence as a self-governing commonwealth within the English empire that parliament would not grant. But then parliament's approach to governing the empire differed little from that of the king it deposed. Remember: parliament acting alone passed the first of the navigation acts.

Whatever confrontation may have been brewing during those years did not actually come until long after restoration of the monarchy in 1660. Frustrated by Massachusetts's continued denial of crown and parliamentary authority over its internal affairs, its expansionist ambitions, its printing of paper money, the widespread smuggling there, and denial of the franchise to those who were not members of local congregational churches, advisers to Charles II recommended that Massachusetts be absorbed into a new super colony. From their perspective the other colonies were but a variation on the Massachusetts as troublemaker theme. They decided that it would better to deal with them together rather than to manage them apart. Their new entity, which combined all of the colonies north and east of the Delaware River into the Dominion of New England, did not finally take form until the reign of James II. New York and New Jersey found themselves joined with Rhode Island, Connecticut, New Hampshire, and the Maine country with Massachusetts; so too the colonists in and around Plymouth who had been resisting absorption into Massachusetts for over sixty years. They were governed by crown-appointed officials, there was no representative assembly, old land titles were reviewed and new land taxes were applied. Customs inspectors and vice-admiralty judges had their authority bolstered, which did not bode well for smugglers.

Chances are that if the Dominion had succeeded, the remaining colonies to the south would have been similarly combined. But the Dominion fell almost before it was erected. It had begun after legal proceedings in London stripped individual colonies of their charters or those charters were simply annulled. In 1689, less than a year after the Dominion had finally been pieced together, it burst apart with uprisings, first in Boston, then in New York. Taking advantage of the Glorious Revolution in England, colonists looking for the opportunity—and excuse—to rise seized the moment. Royally appointed Dominion officials were arrested as local councils of safety took power into their own hands, claiming to act for the people and in defense of the empire as it should have been, not as it was. Assuming that the new monarchs, William and Mary, would not denounce their actions, they proclaimed themselves loyal subjects acting on their behalf as well. Their gamble paid off; the Dominion was dissolved and the individual colonies were restored—though Plymouth was kept within Massachusetts and the Bay Colony had its claim to the Maine country reaffirmed. Those who had overthrown the Dominion denied that they behaved as revolutionaries or that they committed unlawful acts. Rather, they insisted that they had defended their constitutional rights as Englishmen. Not seeking further confrontation and desiring, first and foremost, a restoration of peace in the empire, crown and parliament did not press fine points of the law and the colonists expressed general contentment.

Basic questions about the limits to imperial authority and the extent of local autonomy were put aside for the time being. Whitehall and Westminster would not attempt anything remotely as ambitious thereafter, and yet war came in 1775. What marked the difference between the temporary restoration of harmony in English America in 1689 and its permanent disruption in 1776 was social and political, not constitutional. The issues raised in both instances were the same, although the response on both sides of the Atlantic was different. Simply put, colonial society had reached a maturity by 1776 that it had lacked in 1689. And yet it is notable that political lines could be as blurred in 1776 as they had been in 1689. Not all colonists had objected to the Dominion; not all colonists would embrace independence. To think in terms of clearly delineated English or American positions is to oversimplify the complexities of empire and to ignore the avoidance of constitutional ultimates that characterized the problem-solving approach taken on both sides of the Atlantic.

Imperial Unease

The larger the empire became, the more difficult it was to handle effectively—a function of overseas enterprise in general, not the peculiarities of Britain's approach. For much of the time imperial relations worked well enough. Adam Smith exaggerated when he claimed that Americans prospered despite, not because of, Britain's mercantilism. This is just one area where false dichotomies—misleading either/or propositions—ought to be resisted. The colonists smuggled but they did not disobey all trade laws. They demanded greater autonomy and yet expressed pride in being part of the empire and swore their allegiance to it. Crown and parliament, and the various experts who advised them, rarely turned punitive. They were even convinced that the Dominion of New England had had much to recommend it from the colonial perspective as well as their own.

As tensions mounted in the 1760s there would be colonists who pointed to the Dominion as proof that there had never been an effective community of interests, much less a true imperial family. The long-dead Edward Randolph, whose reports to London about Massachusetts's misbehavior helped launch the Dominion, lived on in some New England minds as an imperial bogeyman. By that same token, memories in London could be long too: of ungrateful colonists who needed to be taught a lesson, and of the danger of doing too little to shape them as well as the drawback of attempting too much.

Issues revolving around the navigation system were mixed in with many others. Boundary disputes, for example, were endemic. During the earliest years of settlement, Virginia and Maryland had clashed over fishing rights and islands in the Chesapeake. Virginia's 1612 charter gave the colony no fixed western boundary; likewise Georgia's in 1732. These so-called "sea-to-sea" charters could cause divisions between colonies and potentially pit Britain against France, to the north and west, and Spain to the west and south. Other colonies had their variations on this theme, with Connecticut and Massachusetts contending with New York over their shared borders. Rival claims over the Vermont country could be even more vexing.

The list could be extended but the point would remain the same. Those boundary disputes would in fact carry over into the early national era. They divided states in the new American union and complicated American relations with foreign powers, just as they had provinces in the empire. Moreover, relations within colonies as well as between colonies could be fractious. The Paxton riots erupted with tensions unleashed in western Pennsylvania after the French and Indian War. The Regulator disturbances in the Carolinas followed not long after. Those who contend that the struggle over who would rule at home was as pronounced as the contest over home rule may exaggerate, but imperial administrators did assume that inter-colonial collaboration in response to unpopular policies coming out of London was most unlikely, given the political and social divisions that marked British America.

Even so, differentiating between colonies—say those supposedly founded for religious purposes and others for economic reasons—ought to be done very carefully. Those who settled Massachusetts and Virginia, often cast as opposites, as colonists were not fundamentally that different. It is not just that spiritual and materialistic motivations could be found in most colonists, regardless of where they chose to settle. For far too long, suggests historian Jack P. Greene, far too much has been made of the distinctions between Puritan New England and the Chesapeake colonies. Massachusetts and Virginia both began as joint stock company enterprises. More important, both brought together notions of the common good, whether through the covenant that bound the religious or the contract that teamed investor with settler. Church membership and corporate involvement both carried obligations as well as opportunities, putting a premium on self-rule even if notions of what was a good return on investment differed. Both Massachusetts and Virginia would evolve governmental forms that had their origins in the founding corporate structure. "Freemen," so called because they bought shares in an England-based investment enterprise, were eventually replaced by freemen with voting and office-holding rights as American settlers.

Almost all of the colonies that chose independence in 1776 had been granted a charter—or charters in succession—at one point or another. And all of those charters more or less guaranteed the settlers within their bounds the rights of Englishmen. On the most fundamental level, charters did not create rights; rather, they recognized rights that Englishmen who became settlers believed they took with them abroad. But what, precisely, could be included within the range of possible rights was always a matter of debate. Did those rights include a representative assembly? Some charters were more specific on that matter than others. Even if an individual colony had an express right to an assembly, could that right be rescinded? The colonial American reading of English common law as it extended to them held that customary practice had legal standing. In other words, traditions long practiced could not be ended by government fiat, even if they had no statutory protection or precedent in case law. And yet the Dominion of New England seemed to say that nothing was beyond the reach of the crown-in-council. When, in the aftermath of the 1772 *Gaspee* affair, there were rumors that Rhode Island and Connecticut might both lose their charters and be combined into a single colony, old fears were easily resurrected.

Even if those assemblies within individual colonies were allowed to stand, what came within their purview? Most were expressly enjoined from passing laws "repugnant" to those of England. But who determined what fell within that forbidden range? Of the eight thousand or so laws passed by colonial assemblies between 1619 and 1776, just over five hundred were disallowed—that is, declared null and void by the crown-in-council. But what mattered most in this arrangement, the fact that the royal disallowance was exercised so infrequently or that it could be exercised at all? For most of their histories, neither Rhode Island nor Connecticut felt compelled to send their laws across the Atlantic for review. Most others colonies behaved in a like manner.

All of the colonies with representative assemblies, from Jamaica and Barbados in the West Indies to Virginia and, well over a century later, to Georgia on the mainland, followed a similar governmental pattern. They did so, not because of some sort of master plan imposed by London, but as a result of introducing the familiar into the strange. It was somehow very English to have a governor as the executive authority; so too a legislative assembly, with an elective lower house and appointed upper house, or with a single house and governor's council that essentially performed the same function as the upper house in other colonies. In many colonial minds those arrangements were the provincial equivalent of the crown, House of Lords, and House of Commons in Britain. Whitehall and Westminster disputed the analogy. In a hierarchical empire, they countered, no colonial government could be anything more than a subordinate unit.

That Britain itself was so attached to the forms—returning to them after attempting an alteration during the Interregnum of 1649–1660—is a reminder that those English forms grew out of time-honored assumptions. To divide power among the one (monarchy), the aristocratic few (the Lords), and the democratic many (the Commons), with their colonial variations, was an Aristotelian notion; likewise the fear that any one of those three, if unchecked by the other two, could devolve into more dangerous forms—monarchy into tyranny, aristocracy into oligarchy, and democracy into anarchy. Those assumptions about political tendencies would survive the Revolution. They were reflected not just in the governmental forms that would eventually be adopted in the new American nation, but also in the explication about their logic provided by John Adams.

And yet the unity of thought that can be traced through political philosophy did not necessarily carry through into politics. Different perspectives would constantly come into play as the British empire in America matured: one group within one colony versus another; one colony versus another; the mainland colonies in general versus the mother country. The possible iterations are too numerous to list here and all contributed to the potential of imperial instability. Ironically, the divisions that caused *intra*-colonial and *inter*-colonial contention would often be laid at the doorstep of crown and parliament by disgruntled colonists and by critics of imperial policy in Britain itself. From Whitehall and Westminster's perspective it was aggravating to be distrusted as the source of problems one moment and then be looked to by disputatious colonists as the court of last resort the next.

The mainland colonies of British North America that turned to revolution in 1776 had benefited immensely from being part of the British empire. Nonetheless there were colonists frustrated by imperial policies that they felt hurt them. Their complaints increased with the policy changes brought following the French and Indian War. What is more, they looked beyond the present policies to anticipate what the next set of changes would bring. As has often been observed about them, they reacted more to tyranny anticipated than to tyranny experienced.

Future revolutionaries in the colonies and their opponents in Britain saw certain changes as inevitable. They also believed in the role of human actors who could shape that change. Loath to say that those in power only delayed or accelerated the inevitable, they—John Adams again standing in as their representative—may have thought that the rise of nations and empires would end in their fall, but they refused to be fatalists. What had brought down Rome might in turn bring down Britain, Adams conceded, but there was a part of him that wanted to think Britain's empire of liberty would fare better. After reluctantly abandoning that hope for the old British empire, he would transfer it to the new American nation.

But we need to remember that before John Adams became a nation founder he had been an imperial reformer. The difficulty of sustaining overseas empire notwithstanding, the Adamses and Franklins of the Revolutionary generation proceeded in the belief that their actions mattered, that they could build a better British empire. So did their adversaries on both sides of the Atlantic, even if they worked from a different perspective. They agreed that the past should guide without binding. They all believed they had a role to play in shaping the empire according to their differing notions of what best served their idealized community. That community included subjects of the crown living in colonies across the ocean who took it as a given that they had inalienable rights, beyond the reach of any government, provincial or imperial. Those assumptions were perfectly natural. They were also potentially disruptive.

Chapter 2

Crippling Mortgages

Wars for Empire

When the first of what would be collectively called the four wars for empire between France and England erupted in 1689, the mainland of North America was not as important to either nation's ambitions as it would be in 1763, when the fourth war ended. Only in that last conflict would North America be the strategic focus for either power. In the first three, the fighting in North America was of limited significance, almost always secondary to more important scenes of action in Europe and adjacent waters. Balance of power considerations lay at the heart of each conflict. The one diplomatic constant in the shifting alliances that occurred over these years is that France was on one side and England (after 1707, Great Britain) on the other. Only with time did the Americas in general, and the North American continent in particular, come to be decisive in determining war objectives. In all four wars the notion of a reciprocal empire would be tested. Sometimes imperial and colonial interests aligned; other times they did not.

Predictably enough, fighting that erupted in Europe between nations with overseas holdings often spread to the American colonies. Even so, there is no perfect correlation between military events on opposite sides of the Atlantic. Colonists attached to one empire living cheek-by-jowl to colonists joined with another sometimes initiated hostilities on their own. Occasionally they made accommodations to avoid following their mother countries into war. As a case in point, English and French settlers shared the island of St. Kitts for nearly a century. Relations were occasionally hostile, with property destroyed and lives lost, but the islanders determined for themselves when and how they would fight. Neither London nor Versailles sanctioned their independent actions. Once the wars for empire began in earnest, it proved impossible to stand apart from them. The island would pass fully to Britain in 1713, in the treaty ending that second war.

Variations on this theme were apparent on the North American mainland as well. The Spanish, French, and English all jockeyed for the most advantageous position, as did Indian tribes caught up in that competition who had ambitions of their own. There were times when the Iroquois, only nominally tied to the English during the early stages of the wars for empire, preferred neutrality to military action against the French and their Algonquian allies. New Yorkers irritated by that behavior might in turn irritate New Englanders who found them to be reluctant partners against the supposed common enemy. Massachusetts authorities could be frustrated with settlers in the Maine country, who too often seemed content to trade illicitly with the French and their Abenaki allies. Inter-colonial frustrations were only compounded once imperial authorities became involved, with their own set of expectations.

The French and the Spanish to the south and west of English settlements could easily have gone to war over rival territorial claims—the Spanish pointed west from St. Augustine beyond Pensacola, the French looking east from New Orleans past Mobile. There was occasional friction and attempts to sway the local tribes, which those tribes often turned to their advantage. But there was nothing to match the fighting that would erupt between the French and English to the north, even before Spain and France were allied under the 1733 Family Compact.

It is too easy to forget that the Anglo-French competition that defined the wars for empire emerged from what had been a much more fluid set of political circumstances. The shifting among alliances and diplomatic maneuvers that went with them defy simple explanation. In the early 1650s both France and Spain had considered an alliance with England under the commonwealth, despite the republicanism there that they found so anathema. England, weighing its options, chose France over Spain. Acting as lord protector, Oliver Cromwell did not realize his dream of an English Caribbean, though Jamaica was captured in 1655 in the subsequent Anglo-Spanish war. The Anglo-French tie did not gain either nation much in the Old World. In the New it helped to mitigate frictions over rival claims in the West Indies and on the mainland of North America. Thus, for many years did the English and French avoid fighting over Acadia, controlled by the French, or over the Hudson Bay operations of the English or their outposts on Newfoundland.

The three Anglo-Dutch trade wars that spanned the 1650s to 1670s spilled across the Atlantic, which led to the loss of New Netherland to England. But conflicting territorial claims in North America were not the primary reason for the fighting. England never recognized the legitimacy of New Netherland. And yet Connecticut engaged in its own foreign policy with the Dutch there, negotiating commercial agreements and resolving boundary disputes. Even Virginians treated with the Dutch and were disappointed when fighting crossed the Atlantic to disrupt their trade. The end of those wars, coupled with the growing importance of the Americas to English and French political ambitions, made it increasingly difficult to keep fighting that began in Europe from spreading across the Atlantic. As borders in Europe became more fixed, the borders of empire abroad became even more contested. With that shifting emphasis, the West Indies and the mainland of North America increasingly took center stage.

Events in Europe tied to the Glorious Revolution triggered the first of the four Anglo-French transoceanic wars, although American disputes were included in the list of mutual grievances. Fighting extended to the colonies but the outcomes were settled among negotiators in Europe, not America, with the primary considerations being European, not American. The most notable fighting in North America was not all that notable. In 1690 an essentially Massachusetts funded, manned, and equipped expedition seized Port Royal in what was then Acadia. The wooden stockade erected to protect a few other wooden structures, defended by fewer than one hundred men, was surrendered without a fight. In the treaty ending the war in 1697, Port Royal became one of the bargaining chips on the negotiating table. The English agreed to return it to the French. In exchange the French recognized the legitimacy of William and Mary as monarchs and Dutch claims to contested lands in the low countries that the Netherlands, England's ally, wanted secured. In this instance the interests of old England and New England diverged rather than converged, testing without destroying the notion of a reciprocal empire. The more important impact was not that of the moment but seven decades later, when leaders of the Revolutionary generation would point to American needs being shunted aside as proof that the empire had never worked.

The Bay colonists, with the help of other New Englanders and New Yorkers, had intended to take both Quebec and Montreal in that first war as well. Their reach exceeded their grasp. If they had succeeded, then the history of Anglo-French relations in North America—perhaps even in the larger world—would have been dramatically different. As the historian Jeremy Black has argued, the role of contingent developments and the possibility of alternative outcomes ought to be kept in mind whenever cause and effect explanations are offered. For example, Quebec had fallen to an enterprising English adventurer, David Kirke, in 1629. Kirke did his filibustering during the reign of Charles I, before American affairs mattered all that much to Anglo-French relations. The English government did not disavow Kirke's actions but it did consent to return Quebec (and Acadia, which Kirke, his brothers, and the Scottish adventurer William Alexander had taken) to France, in return for other considerations closer to home. If policy makers in London had accorded American affairs more weight, then the history of New France would have been much shorter and the great wars for empire might never have occurred, or at least followed a different course.

With hindsight we could say, misleadingly, that New France was simply a long time falling. In all four of the wars, Quebec was the most compelling target. Seizing it would be the first step toward complete French expulsion—long an Anglo-American dream. By the fourth and final conflict the population disparity between the rivals was more pronounced than ever: over two million British Americans as opposed to perhaps seventy thousand French Canadians, both with indispensable Indian allies who held the local balance of power. The French could never muster enough resources to even conquer New York by advancing down the Lake Champlain corridor, though leaders in Quebec wished they could have. During individual wars they did take the offensive. But overall, in grand strategy, they were always on the defensive, trying their best to hang on to the loyalty of allied tribes, the lucrative fur trade that those Indian alliances made possible, and lands extending from New Orleans in an arc from the lower Mississippi basin through the Ohio country to the Great Lakes and out to the St. Lawrence. It was an expanse so huge, so unmapped, that even as late as the fourth war the governor of New France in Quebec and the governor of Louisiana in New Orleans could not be certain where one province began and the other ended.

If, in the first war, England's imperial and colonial interests had too often diverged, in the second they occasionally converged. Massachusetts mounted another attack on Port Royal, succeeded again, and had the satisfaction of seeing part of Acadia sliced off from New France and incorporated within the British empire as Nova Scotia, with a new center of local power eventually built at Halifax. It was not that London had somehow become more attuned to Boston's preferences. Rather, Britain had fared much better in this conflict and could drive a tougher bargain at the peace table. Not only were negotiators able to demand a portion of Acadia, but they were also able to insist that Spain, France's ally, give them trade privileges long denied them with Spain's American colonies. That included a piece of the slave trade that the English had been craving since the days of Hawkins and Drake.

And yet in the third war the problem of divergence returned. This time the source of imperial and colonial contention would be the massive stone fortress at Louisbourg. It had been built on Cape Breton Island to secure New France's east flank in a way that Port Royal, now lost, never could. Though the Royal Navy played a hand, Massachusetts spearheaded the successful 1745 siege that dropped Louisbourg into Britain's lap. Resentment in the Bay Colony ran deep when, in 1748, as a diplomatic bargaining chip, Louisbourg was returned to France in order to better secure Britain's empire elsewhere in the world. Louisbourg, then, would be added to the list of grievances compiled by Revolutionary Era protestors as they sought proof of the empire's perennial failings. Writing anonymously for a London newspaper in 1770, Benjamin Franklin would be one member of the chorus of critics who cried out that the colonists, ever loyal, had been badly used in that war, as they had been in others.

Louisbourg fell a second time, in 1758, during the last of the wars, to a markedly different force. Colonists were involved but the bulk of the fighting was done by British regulars and the British navy. Most of the funding came from parliament. The results there anticipated how Quebec would fall the next year and Montreal the year after that. The colonies played a decidedly subordinate if essential role as New France finally teetered and fell. Joined in common cause for the moment, cultural clashes and political friction could be overlooked while Britons and Americans shared the elation of victory. France lost everything but two small islands off of Newfoundland in its once huge North American empire, which could be used as fishing bases but must remain unfortified. New France proper passed to Britain, as did the Ohio country and virtually all of the territory between the Appalachians and the Mississippi. New Orleans and its immediate environs passed to Spain, which, because of its last-minute alliance with France, turned over the Floridas to Britain. France also lost ground in the Mediterranean, in Africa, in India, and several islands in the West Indies. It could have been worse. Britain returned other holdings that it had taken during the war: Guadeloupe and Martinique to France, and Havana and Manila to Spain. It kept four other Caribbean islands that it had captured. Colonial Americans were understandably proud to be connected to what had emerged as the greatest maritime power in the world.

But ultimately, as the Comte de Vergennes had predicted, with the French gone, good feelings faded. All too often familiarity had bred contempt. With Britons and British Americans thrown together in larger numbers over an extended period for the first time, fissures appeared in their shared final war effort. Frustrations grew among British general officers, who found that colonial legislatures could not be ordered about or be relied upon to provide troops and supplies. British field officers distrusted ill-disciplined American militia. British naval officers saw their press gangs resisted in colonial seaports and their ocean-going patrols pursued colonists trading illicitly with the French. Colonists who resented their inferior status in the partnership and felt the scorn too often directed at them by Britons had their own complaints. Whatever resentments that had built up during the war had no chance to dissipate because, again as Vergennes predicted, postwar policies would accentuate them.

Bigger Empire, Higher Costs

The fourth and final conflict had escalated far beyond its modest beginnings in 1754. The flashpoint was Anglo-French disputes over the rightful title to the Ohio country and a test of whose Indian alliances were most decisive. The French had not contested the titular Iroquois connection to Britain but they did reject the Iroquois claim to suzerainty over tribes in that vast region. France's assertion that its territory extended all the way from the Great Lakes to New Orleans could not be reconciled with Britain's general claim, as expressed most ambitiously in Virginia's sea-to-sea charter over much of the same land, and the ambitions of the Ohio Company and other investors in western lands. Spain did not really accept either nation's claim but was in no position to interfere. George Washington would first become known for his involvement in this Anglo-French dispute, beginning as a twenty-one-year-old Virginia militia major sent by his governor to tell the French to desist in their activities around the forks of the Ohio River. Washington was swept up in the quickly expanding confrontation.

And yet, at the outset neither the British nor the French thought the contest consequential enough to require a formal declaration of war, even as they prepared for battle. In that sense they backed into hostilities the same way they had in the previous conflict, when Britain fought for years in the Caribbean against first Spain and then France without a declaration of war. In 1754 Anglo-American strategy called for conquest; French strategy, to prevent it. Initially that conquest meant driving the French back from western Pennsylvania, out of New York, and out of the remnant of settled Acadia. Eventually it meant conquest of New France itself. Braddock's march into western Pennsylvania during the early stage was thus part of a much larger, more ambitious British effort. Originally plans had called for a southwestern campaign, with Anglo-American forces joined by Catawbas and Cherokees to secure the Carolina frontier at one end, and a campaign to take Acadia at the other. New York stood as the vital center, with designs on Fort Niagara to the far west and Crown Point on Lake Champlain. Braddock's assault on Fort Duquesne was intended to be a branch off that larger push. The southern campaign did not get off the ground; likewise for the attack on Niagara. The effort in the Champlain area did not fail as miserably as Braddock's. Still, the only real success came in Acadia.

Britain's declaration of war in 1756 did not bring with it rapid North American success. That declaration was precipitated as much by Old World concerns as New, fueled by exaggerated rumors of French plans for a cross-channel invasion of England and shock at the French assault on Minorca in the undeclared war that had spread to the Mediterranean. With some aid from home, New France held its own for two years before it gave way to the overwhelming strength of a determined Britain. Parliament, led by William Pitt, committed resources on a scale not seen before, not just to secure British claims on the mainland of North America, but to strengthen Britain's position in the West Indies, in the Mediterranean, and in India, and to stabilize the balance of power on the European continent. Pitt's ambitious war did not involve some sort of fundamental reconceptualization of empire: commercial wealth and territorial gain overseas had always been linked with controlling power relations closer to home. Even so, there were those in London who worried that pushing farther west into the North American interior ought to be better planned and coordinated, so that the autonomous tendencies of the seaboard colonies would not be repeated farther inland—and even further from London's control.

Military and diplomatic success in this worldwide conflict came at a high price, both in a literal sense—deficit spending that doubled the national debt—and in a more figurative one, as imperial administrators were pressed to decide how to distribute increased costs around that larger empire. It is not as if they had any breathing room between the end of the war and the restoration of peace to set their priorities. Leaders in London could not be sure until well into 1763 that Hanover, ancestral home of George III, was secure and the continent out of danger. Only then did Frederick II of Prussia, with behind-the-scenes British assistance, fight back attacks from three directions: by the French, Austrians, and Russians. An uprising among tribes in the Ohio country labeled Pontiac's Rebellion came before the 1763 peace treaty between Britain and France was even signed. An uprising on the Carolina frontier involving erstwhile Cherokee allies had erupted before Montreal's surrender three years before that. The royal proclamation creating a line running down the Appalachians to temporarily separate white settlements from tribal lands was issued in October 1763, as the fighting in the Ohio country between Fort Detroit, to the west, and Fort Pitt, to the east, still raged.

It is interesting that, in the midst of this frontier crisis, General Jeffrey Amherst, the British commander-in-chief, thought it would be wise to station at least a few troops along the seaboard in case the colonists there became restive as a result of any unpopular postwar policies introduced from London. By the time that British regulars, with the assistance of some militia and Indian allies, crushed Pontiac's Rebellion, parliament, under the leadership of George Grenville had indeed begun an attempt at imperial reform.

Grenville has ever since been a convenient whipping boy for Britain's postwar policy failure. But he was no fool, nor were those who sided with him. All knew that raising taxes anywhere in the empire—mother country as well as colonies—would be unpopular. An experienced politician, Grenville understood that if he attempted to close the gap between imperial ideal and colonial reality, he took a calculated risk. In the rewards and punishment system that accompanied governing the empire, he needed to please more interest groups than he offended. From his perspective—and that of the solid majority in both houses of parliament who supported him, offending colonists posed less of a problem than alienating Britons. The changed strategic circumstances brought with French expulsion actually provided an opportunity to try new policies being contemplated long before the latest war even erupted.

Neither Grenville nor his successors over the next decade had any illusions about paying off the nation's debt. Debt management, not debt elimination, was their goal. What is more, the policies that Grenville introduced had been considered before the war even began, which should serve as a caution against making oversimplified cause-and-effect relationships. That is to say, postwar policies did not simply flow from postwar circumstances. In some instances the end of the war provided the occasion for a new policy, not the underlying impetus for it. With the unsettled markets and falling prices that came on the heels of the war, Grenville's timing for new taxes could not have been worse.

Given how often Grenville's objectives are misrepresented and the amounts involved misstated, setting the record straight means reviewing the imperial balance sheet. Britain's national debt in 1763 had risen to roughly £140 million, a doubling of the total as it stood in 1754. To keep that amount from growing even larger the Treasury would need to increase revenue significantly. Without new taxes, revenue would be roughly £10 million annually. Expenses would exceed that amount by £3 million or so. That £13 million total could be divided into operating costs, domestic and international, at £8 million per annum, and paying £5 million in annual interest on the overall debt.

In Britain, tax revenues were generated from three basic sources: the land or hearth tax on property, an excise tax on domestically produced goods such as beer and ale, and then customs duties connected to trade in the empire. By 1763 the excise tax generated the most revenue, customs duties came second, and the land tax, once the highest, had become a distant third—a commentary on the rising value of commerce and the increasing amount of vendible goods being produced in Britain's growing economy.

By contrast, parliament's only source of colonial revenue came from customs duties. No imperial administrator thought that the individual colonial legislatures could be called on to make the same requisitions among their inhabitants in peace as they had during war. Before the war disrupted trade, revenue actually collected amounted to well under £3000 a year—less than what it cost to maintain the bureaucratic apparatus for collecting those duties. Imperial administrators advising the crown and parliament estimated that a phenomenal £500,000 a year was lost in colonial smuggling and a fair amount of that in trade with the enemy. Add to that the problem of determining what could be considered a fair sharing of wartime costs. From the Treasury's perspective, the colonies should have been grateful that they were reimbursed for some of their wartime expenses, to the tune of over £1 million. From the perspective of some colonists, since that only covered half of their total expenditure, it was not enough. Here was a problem that was as political as it was financial: the idealized imperial family had become dysfunctional.

The principal immediate postwar cost in North America would be the posting of troops on the frontier to enforce the Proclamation Line. Those troops were expected to prevent white settlers from moving west, to remove those who had taken up residence across the line, and to block unlicensed merchants from trading with the tribes there. Investors in western lands were not formally stripped of their titles but, for the present, whatever claims they had were held in abeyance. Allowing for twenty regiments to perform that frontier duty—roughly ten thousand men—would mean an annual expense to London of well over £200,000. With plans to increase the number of vice-admiralty courts and strengthen the customs service, total costs could potentially jump to twice that amount.

Imperial accountants knew that Britons paid higher per capita taxes than colonists. Modern estimates are that the average British family paid about 20% of household income in taxes and its North American counterpart perhaps 1%. Adding another couple of percent to the British tax burden was one thing; adding a like amount to the colonists would double, even treble the total. Grenville and his colleagues could anticipate that colonists would protest both the amount and the source of the tax increase, which would be parliament rather than their own representative assemblies. That was one reason why Grenville did not intend American-generated customs duties to be applied to anything other than American expenses. Moreover, he did not expect to bring in more than £100,000 in new revenue over the first couple of years, so that the colonists would be eased into the new emphasis on stricter enforcement and higher revenue. Withal, he miscalculated—badly, as did those who supported him, their king, George III, included.

Failure Compounded

Two acts that parliament passed in 1764 were directed at British America: the so-called "Sugar Act" and a Currency Act. They were paired with two more added the following year: a Quartering Act and a Stamp Act. Each was a component part of a larger program; each had its political as well as its financial side.

The American Revenue Act or "Sugar Act" came first. It enlarged and extended the Molasses Act of 1733, reducing the duty set on foreign molasses from 6 to 3 pence per gallon, but with the understanding that the law, long ignored, would now be enforced. The duty on foreign sugar went up; foreign rum was banned altogether. New duties were placed on other trade items and the list of enumerated goods that needed to pass through Britain or certain approved ports was lengthened as well. A related decision at the Admiralty Office provided for a new vice-admiralty court in Halifax to hear appeals in smuggling and other trade law cases, and the customs service received a boost: inspectors could be awarded as much as a third of the proceeds from public auctions resulting from their confiscations that were upheld in court. Royal Navy officers could also enjoy a share, if they made a seizure at sea. So could governors and even the royal exchequer. All of this would someday be condemned as "customs racketeering," as if it introduced some new form of governmental corruption. Actually the notion of profiting from public office was common on both sides of the Atlantic and would even be carried into the new national government set up by the United States in 1776.

The Currency Act forbade the printing of paper money in the colonies. Paper money had been allowed on and off over the years, and proved useful during the most recent war but it could prove destabilizing if it continued. The imperial economy had already been disrupted by the fighting and the unavoidable confusion over exchange rates that accompanied colonial paper competing with specie coined in Britain and on the continent could potentially worsen the postwar downturn. Purchases could still be made on credit, however. Trade would have been almost impossible without merchants trusting each other and, after all, the purpose of reform was to enhance legitimate commerce, not curtail it. Thus the bounties offered in separate legislation for flax and hemp to bolster the production of naval stores, the prohibitory stick still being combined with the promotional carrot.

The Quartering Act of the next year extended to the colonies certain provisions of the Mutiny Act passed for Britain. Under it colonial governments were expected to provide barracks, either in unoccupied public buildings or rented space in private buildings, including unoccupied houses. Colonial authorities were also expected to provide basic provisions. Nothing was said about obliging individual homeowners to rent space in places they occupied. Doing so would have raised the specter of an unconstitutional violation of the spirit of the 1689 Bill of Rights, which colonists assumed applied to them—as did Britons who might have otherwise been unsympathetic to colonial protests about housing troops among civilians during peacetime. Furthermore, deserters could not be looked for in private houses without a search warrant. Even so, this Act rubbed a sore spot going back to the late war, when British commanders haggled with colonial leaders about housing and providing for regular troops.

The Stamp Act was by far the most ambitious piece of legislation in Grenville's program and by far the most upsetting to the colonists. There would be over thirty different types of stamps, with stamped (meaning embossed) sheets ranging from as little as 3 pence apiece to as much as £10. Almost all printed matter was involved, from playing cards to newspapers to legal documents to college diplomas. Stamped paper had been required for various items in Britain since 1694. Colonial legislatures had fallen back on stamped paper during the war as a revenue-raising device. Grenville presented this new act as simply an extension of the navigation system, which the proposed prosecution of violators before vice-admiralty judges rather than in common-law courts underscored. But no other piece of imperial legislation stirred as much resistance among the colonists. They decried it as a new type of direct tax, unconstitutional in nature and excessive in its demands on the colonial pocketbook. That lawyers, printers, and clergymen (with their published sermons) were among those most directly affected did not help Grenville's cause.

Grenville's ministry fell in the summer of 1765 before the Stamp Act went into effect on November 1. It fell more because of internecine crown and parliamentary political disputes than because of adverse reaction to the Stamp Act among the colonists and London merchants upset by the disruption to trade. Before the Stamp Act became dead letter law, the various types of protest that would mark colonial agitation against unpopular imperial policies over the next decade all manifested themselves: official remonstrances from local legislatures, essays by individuals printed as pamphlets or run in newspapers, public protests that could devolve into mob violence, boycotts of British goods and attempts to stimulate "home manufactures," and extra-legal meetings marked, most notably, by the Stamp Act Congress in New York during October.

Repeal of the Stamp Act in March 1766 had been accompanied with a Declaratory Act that nicely captured London's combination of assertiveness and evasiveness. The Declaratory Act claimed parliament's authority to legislate for the colonists "in all cases whatsoever" but deliberately left out the word "tax." The Marquess of Rockingham, who headed the new ministry that replaced Grenville's, hoped thereby to move past disagreements of the moment and henceforth take a "let sleeping dogs lie" approach to imperial administration. In other words, parliament should raise revenue and regulate trade as necessary, but without stirring up constitutional issues or provoking political disputes. The Declaratory Act was ambiguous enough that defenders of the empire could consider it assertive, even as critics of the empire (temporarily, at least) accepted it as conciliatory. Equally as interesting as the omission of the word "tax" was the announcement that any colonial protests that had questioned parliament's legitimate authority would be ignored as "utterly null and void"—as if the issue had never been raised. Apparently living in denial seemed preferable to asking political questions that had no satisfactory answers.

Rockingham saw to a further modification of the Sugar Act, reducing the molasses duty across the board, with no distinction made between foreign or domestic sources. He hoped that West Indies producers would look past their loss of a monopoly against foreign competitors and accept the lower duty. He also hoped that colonial consumers would appreciate the lower duty and accept the reality of stricter enforcement. Beyond that, he had no major plans for change.

His ministry lasted only a year. It fell, as had Grenville's, for reasons apart from imperial administration. His successor, William Pitt, admired by many colonists as the man who drove the French out of North America, had been elevated to the House of Lords and took little part in the new programs that emerged in the spring of 1767. Charles Townshend, chancellor of the exchequer, assumed the lead. He in effect picked up where Grenville left off, though he mistakenly thought he could avoid the hue and cry raised by the Stamp Act. His new Revenue Act added more items to the list of dutied exports to the colonies, tea being the most important among them. Better enforcement was promoted through the creation of a Boston-based customs board and yet more emendations to the vice-admiralty court system.

Townshend's program caused as much contention as had Grenville's. Disgruntled colonists protested against the revenue-raising element of it, though, from London's perspective, they had little ground for complaint. The hoped for £100,000 of 1765 had been left behind as unrealistic, given American propensities to evade the law. Townshend, who died of typhus just as protests began to be heard, would have been content with half that amount. And indeed, within a year some £30,000 began to flow in through customs revenue annually. That amount did not even begin to cover the costs of keeping troops on the frontier but it more than met the expense of the enlarged civilian bureaucracy charged with enforcing the navigation acts. Only about half of the increased revenue came from the new items added in Townshend's act. None came from tea because all of the proceeds generated by the tea duty found their way back to the East India Company.

The company's fortunes were inextricably tied to the sale of tea, which accounted for perhaps 90% of its revenue. Crown and parliament were advised that colonists on the mainland of North America consumed several hundred thousand pounds of tea annually. Most, perhaps even three-quarters of it, they obtained illegally through smuggling with the Dutch, who by and large obtained their tea from the same Chinese sources used by the company. The company was inefficiently, even corruptly, run. But such was the pressure to succeed that it paid dividends to investors, many of whom sat in parliament, even when no profits had been generated. To keep the company solvent, parliament offered it "drawbacks"—essentially rebates—on the duties it was supposed to be paying on tea, as it occasionally did to others involved in overseas trade.

Colonists protested against a system that empowered parliament to grant a trade monopoly allowing one private enterprise such an advantage over others. That there would have been, for all intents and purposes, no British empire in the East without the company was not their concern. Parliament passed a new Act in 1773, under yet another ministry, to assist the company, after the other elements of Townshend's 1767 Revenue Act had been repealed three years before. With the company still insolvent, the new Act was designed to better secure its position in the empire. Only merchants licensed by the company would be allowed to sell its tea. New price supports did make company tea competitive with that smuggled in illicitly. Even so, the pro-company policy kept tea duties high on the colonial list of grievances.

That Townshend's desire to create a civil list was not abandoned at the same time as partial repeal only added to the aggravation. Creating a civil list to secure the salaries of royal appointees such as governors and free them from the control of colonial legislatures had long been a dream of imperial administrators. Townshend, for one, had been seeking the right moment to introduce the civil list for well over a decade, even before the French and Indian War.

Adverse colonial reaction to the Townshend program stirred even greater concern at Whitehall and Westminster than had protests against the Stamp Act—but ultimately *because* of the Stamp Act. Legislatures again passed protest resolutions; essayists again penned their objections; local manufactures were again touted and British imports boycotted. All that was lacking was a second extra-legal inter-colonial gathering.

There was a cumulative effect to political thinking on both sides of the Atlantic, among imperial administrators as well as among colonial protesters. The king spoke out more directly against American civil disobedience in 1768 than he had in 1766 *because* of what had happened in 1765. He supported the dispatch of troops to Boston that same year even though the rioting was less destructive then than it had been against the Stamp Act. Interestingly enough, Britons unsympathetic to American protests could have frowned at the stationing of soldiers among civilians in peacetime, condemning it as a violation of the principles upheld by the Glorious Revolution. Grenville, who considered recommending that troops be sent to enforce his program, opposed sending troops to enforce Townshend's. He understood that any attempt to impose the imperial will that was successfully resisted by colonial opponents further weakened imperial authority. Sure enough, the Boston "Massacre" of 1770, which resulted in the withdrawal of British troops from Boston proper, would prove his point.

But then we should think of London's attempts to control Boston as proof of the difficulty of restoring something that was lost; indeed, the difficulty of attempting to create a sense of imperial superiority over local authority that had never really existed. What legal historian John Phillip Reid argued for Boston—that protesters there used local political and governmental control to resist, by law, any extension of imperial authority—could be applied to other towns in other provinces as well.

Every bit as important as Boston's successful stand against the presence of troops among civilians in peacetime was Providence's position on the HMS *Gaspee*, a Royal Navy schooner that patrolled Rhode Island waters in search of smugglers. As a direct assault on imperial authority nothing else quite matched it. In June 1772 a group of locals boarded the *Gaspee*, which had run aground in a river just above Narragansett Bay. The commander was shot by the boarders, rowed ashore with his crew, and the schooner was burned to the waterline. London authorized a halfhearted investigation into the affair. In a conspiracy of silence and collusion that reached all the way to the governor's office, Rhode Islanders thwarted any attempt to bring the guilty to trial. No one was ever arrested much less prosecuted for the offense. Instead of colonists being intimidated into obedience, the inquiry furthered efforts at inter-colonial cooperation to protest imperial oppression.

The Boston Tea Party of 16 December 1773 should be considered in that context—as merely the precipitating event for, not the underlying cause of, what concerned colonists condemned as the Coercive or Intolerable Acts. Taken as an individual case, the dumping of privately owned tea into Boston harbor, even if that tea was the property of the parliamentary-licensed East India Company, did not reach the level of resistance to imperial authority as the Boston "Massacre" or the sinking of the *Gaspee*. It was the event as a symbolic embodiment that mattered most, not the event itself.

In a series of retaliatory acts passed between March and June 1774, parliament first closed the port of Boston to general commerce until the province and town agreed to reimburse the East India Company for the cost of the destroyed tea. That reimbursement never came. Parliament also passed a more demanding Quartering Act—though, as before, individual homeowners were not obliged to lodge any troops without compensation. Troops would subsequently be returned to Boston, this time under General Thomas Gage, who was made governor of the province even as he retained his post as North American army commander-in-chief. The Administration of Justice Act made it possible for any imperial official, civilian, or military accused of a capital crime in the colonies to request a change of venue to England. It was never implemented.

All of the new laws combined a desire to both punish and reform, a desire seen most especially in the Massachusetts Government Act. Under this statute, parliament altered the charter without a legal proceeding to set it aside—that action itself was a threat to what colonists thought of as fundamental law. It changed the way members of the governor's council and judges were chosen and removed; likewise for local justices of the peace and sheriffs. All effectively became royal appointees, holding their posts at the sufferance of the governor or of the king who placed him over them. The new Act even altered the rules for calling town meetings. Parliament's objective was to change the balance of power within the province, to embolden the loyal—in effect, to support the obedient majority that imperial administrators felt had been intimidated into silence by a determined disobedient minority. Empower the loyal, disempower the disloyal, and peace and harmony should be restored; that was the hope behind the legislation.

Lord North, who headed the ministry, knew, as had Grenville before him, that he took a calculated risk with any punitive colonial policy. From his perspective this was not a hardline approach. The troops were no more an army of occupation in 1774 than they had been in 1768. He had no intention of having colonists arrested and tried for treason, though the king's solicitor general and attorney general ruled there were grounds for so doing. But, having come into office in 1770 pushing partial repeal of the Townshend program, North now felt that he had no choice—that Massachusetts had been taken over by the disloyal and disingenuous, and that other colonies would follow suit if he did not act. As with Grenville before, so with him now: the risk of doing too little outweighed the risk of attempting too much.

Conspiracy theories, always popular in the Anglo-American world, became even more widespread. Each side had its proof. That the Quebec Act could be caught up in the dispute is an indication that different priorities were becoming irreconcilable. The Quebec Act passed parliament in the same session as the four Acts noted above. From the perspective of members in the Lords and the Commons, it dealt with an unrelated issue: the need for a more permanent governmental arrangement in what had once been New France. A few at Westminster, like Edmund Burke, warned their colleagues that they misunderstood the emerging American state of mind. The very components of the Quebec Act intended to mollify the Francophone population there alienated the Anglophones to the south. A representative assembly, which had never been part of New France's governmental structure, was left out. The old French legal system, which differed greatly from English common-law practices, was essentially kept in place. Catholicism was to be tolerated, practiced openly alongside Anglicanism. The old Ohio country was included within an enlarged Quebec's jurisdiction.

This last provision in particular galled investors and settlers anticipating an opening to trans-Appalachian development. They knew that the 1763 Proclamation Line had not created some sort of permanent Indian homeland and that London mixed a genuine concern for the natives with a desire to continue controlled western settlement by migrating whites. The Vandalia Company was formed after the line had been drawn, with interests in the same general area as the older Ohio Company. Benjamin Franklin became a member. Yet another group, Franklin among them, explored the possibility of a new colony in that same area to be named Pittsylvania, in honor of the man who led Britain to victory over France. Other investors— Franklin among them too—had hoped to receive land grants farther west in the Illinois country, reaching to the east bank of the Mississippi River. These companies and others included investors in Britain, not just in the colonies. All of these groups were hopeful because the Proclamation Line had been partially erased in 1768. Settlers spilling over the Blue Ridge mountains into western Virginia and Kentucky lands would precipitate Lord Dunmore's War in October 1774, before the ink was even dry on the Quebec Act. That Dunmore, Virginia's royally appointed governor, could prosecute a war that potentially put him at odds with Whitehall and Westminster gives a hint of how complex the politics of empire could be.

From the perspective of too many colonists along the eastern seaboard as well as on the western frontier, being responsive to the preferences of Montreal and Quebec was not an example of imperial flexibility, of being adaptable, tailoring imperial policy to local need. Rather, it stood as a bellwether of pending tyranny—of designs to curtail colonial rights. Distrust—Britons of Americans, Americans of Britons—was poisoning transatlantic relations. Two centuries down the road, Henry Kissinger would advise Americans of the Cold War generation to appreciate linkage in their approach to world affairs: to see that the seemingly disconnected are in fact connected, and to understand that small events could have larger consequences. But what Britons and Americans engaged in by 1774 was lumping rather than linkage. Seeing connections where they only existed in their own minds, they interpreted imperial policies and colonial reactions to them in an unforgiving manner. Too many of them were eliminating the psychological middle ground and paving the way for bloody confrontation.

Chapter 3

Rival Identities

Reluctant Revolutionaries

Samuel Adams has come down to us as the American Revolution personified, as if he in some way willed the independent nation into existence while fellow colonists dithered. Leader of the Boston town meeting, member of the Sons of Liberty, he has been imagined as the man in a red cloak who orchestrated the Boston "Massacre." In even more imaginative renditions he has been credited with firing, unseen, the first shot of April 19, 1775. That is the stereotype; the reality is that while he may have been predicting some sort of confrontation as early as 1768 he did not clearly advocate a war for independence until well after the bloodletting at Lexington and Concord. In between he had been one of many hoping for a stronger American union within the British empire, not a nation independent from it. If something were not done to improve relations, he feared that "this unhappy contest" between Britain and America would "end in Rivers of Blood." When, in 1773, he called for an "American commonwealth," he meant greater intercolonial unity within the empire, not a nation apart. Ironically, before the shooting started, he spent more time trying to head off a confrontation leading to the very revolution he has come to symbolize.

Between 1763 and 1776 there were many colonists like Samuel Adams who moved reluctantly from protest to revolt to revolution. Some who led as reformers balked at revolt and rejected revolution. Some who moved more easily from protest to revolt nonetheless hoped that revolt would not require revolution. Daniel Dulany, a Baltimore lawyer whose widely read pamphlet criticized Grenville's program, fell into that first category; John Dickinson, famous as the "Pennsylvania Farmer" who condemned Townshend's program, fell into the second.

Finding it impossible to pin down precisely the number of those who supported the Revolution and those who were opposed, historians often fall back on John Adams's estimate, offered many years later. Adams divided the colonial population into equal thirds: patriots, loyalists, and neutralists. No doubt the greatest concentration of patriots as a percentage in the overall population could be found in New England. Virginia too was essentially patriot country. Elsewhere the number of loyalists could rival patriots. In New York there may have been as many who fought for the king as against him over the course of the war that erupted in 1775. Given that the fighting came at different times to different places, choosing a side could be postponed. Some colonists switched sides; even more preferred not to choose at all, if possible. For many it was not. As the colonies left the empire to become states in the new nation, they sought to separate those they could trust from those they could not by imposing loyalty oaths. Quakers were often able to avoid oath taking but few others could. The categories of those required to take oaths, and the penalties for those who refused or subsequently broke them, varied from state to state. The Continental Congress did not interfere, even after it became the national government.

Trying to identify the exact point at which the colonial protestor became an American Revolutionary can easily become an exercise in futility. Doing so for Benjamin Franklin might at first glance seem to be easier than for Samuel Adams because Franklin left so much more evidence for us to analyze. And yet Franklin's biographers differ, some seeing the future revolutionary emerging as early as 1768, others only in 1775, as he prepared to leave London for Philadelphia. With Franklin as with Adams there is the problem of differentiating between what he predicted and what he preferred.

It becomes more complicated still when we remember that all of the Revolutionary leaders—like their adversarial counterparts in Britain— believed that no human construct lasts forever and that perspectives change, even within a single lifetime. Franklin said as much in testimony he offered to the House of Commons in February 1766. He had been called there as an expert witness to testify on American attitudes about imperial authority and why so many colonists objected to the Stamp Act. His observations are not important because he influenced the policy leading to repeal; the Rockingham ministry had already decided on that. Nor did the distinction that he made between types of taxes levied by parliament raise eyebrows; others had made the same distinction before him. Rather, his testimony is important as a commentary on popular psychology—*and* as an attempt to warn his listeners of the potential consequences if they misunderstood what a dispute over stamped paper in the colonies portended for the imperial future.

Acting, in effect, as a witness for the prosecution with the Stamp Act serving as the accused, Franklin fielded questions for well over two hours. Some came from members of the Commons sympathetic to repeal who thought parliament had overstepped its bounds. Some came from those who were convinced that parliament had acted properly. Franklin's urging of caution applied to both. One questioner asked Franklin if he thought military force could be used to impose the Stamp Act. Franklin replied no and added that if troops were sent, "they will not find a rebellion; they may indeed make one." In other words, British soldiers among American civilians caused more problems than they solved, raising constitutional issues best left alone. Another asked if the colonists could be relied on to assist Britain should a new war erupt in another part of the world. Franklin offered this qualified yes: "They are zealous for the honour and prosperity of this nation, and, while they are well used, will always be ready to support it, as far as their little power goes." What he left unsaid should have been clear to those listening closely, to wit: American loyalty was conditional, not absolute. It would be based on how well the colonists themselves thought they were being treated. In their world their opinion trumped that of the crown and parliament, and Franklin warned that he could not predict what their reaction to any given policy might be. They could be expected to resist anything that they considered unfair or unconstitutional. His advice would prove to be all too well founded over the next decade.

Mixed Messages

British and American historians often echo each other in dismissing Britain's leadership in the decade leading up to the outbreak of hostilities. In this view, the Stamp Act stands out as the most foolish of Whitehall and Westminster's many ill-considered choices after the French and Indian War. That characterization is a variation on the "blundering generation" of politicians explanation for the coming of the American Civil War. In both views, issues were not so complicated or problems so intractable that some sort of solution could not have been found. The failing, then, was more personal than institutional, the British empire being no more inherently unwieldy in 1775 than the American nation would be in 1861.

In Britain, four ministries quickly came and went between 1763 and 1770. The next in line, under Lord North, though lasting twelve years, is belittled by some as the worst of the lot, longevity only extending the imbecility. And, according to this perspective, all of these ministers served a king of limited intellect and autocratic tendencies. Actually George III was not unusually inept or obsessed with protecting monarchical prerogative. He was certainly not the tyrant of Thomas Paine's *Common Sense*. Nor were the men who led his government simply incompetent. Could more talented leaders have implemented better policies? Perhaps, but that takes us into the realm of counterfactual history and runs the danger of minimizing how difficult keeping the empire together would have been for anyone on the throne or in either house of parliament.

No one in a position of authority over the empire doubted that Britain was sovereign and the colonies subordinate, or that parliament ruled supreme, in the realm and in the dominions beyond. At the same time, by the American Revolutionary Era no political leader in Britain would have advocated a government without limits or a king who ruled by divine right. Those who respected the king as lawgiver also saw him as bound by law. Those who viewed him as a component part of parliament rather than an independent agent also saw parliament itself as limited in its legitimate reach. Government, they agreed, did not create rights; rather, it determined what natural rights were recognized under positive law. That basic understanding had been carried across the Atlantic by colonists in the previous century and their descendants would keep it when they started creating their own national and state governments.

Still, within that broader understanding there existed a large range of policy possibilities when it came to running the empire. Three ministers in succession reflected those differences. George Grenville, who headed the government from 1763 to 1765, did not doubt that parliament had the authority and the need to tax the colonies directly. For him the Stamp Act was like any other act passed by parliament; in this case, it just happened to apply specifically to the Americans. The Marquess of Rockingham, who succeeded Grenville, agreed with him on parliament's authority to tax but disagreed on the need. For Rockingham, the Stamp Act had been unwise, but not unconstitutional. For William Pitt, who in 1766 followed Rockingham's short-lived ministry, the Stamp Act had been both unconstitutional and unwise. He rejected the authority claimed by parliament to pass it and the financial and political need to do so as well. Pitt—by then Earl of Chatham in the House of Lords—made a distinction between taxation and legislation that Grenville and Rockingham did not, nor would the Duke of Grafton who succeeded Chatham in 1768, or North who came in two years after that. For Chatham, taxes were a gift of the people and thus distinct from the general run of legislation. He supported the colonial American insistence that taxation required representation and rejoiced, he said, when they had resisted the Stamp Act.

Townshend's Revenue Act, introduced during Chatham's ministry, does not prove that Chatham, away from Westminster and ill at the time, had allowed an inconsistency to creep in; it was not legislation that contradicted his constitutional position. For him Townshend's new duties were not a direct tax, as the Stamp Act had been. Townshend had simply added new trade items that would be subject to duties. Here is proof that Chatham and American protestors did not think alike, however much he may have condemned the Stamp Act or the evasive language of Rockingham's Declaratory Act. Chatham did not support colonial resistance to all navigation laws passed by parliament and he was emphatic that any colonial action calling into question Britain's sovereignty or parliament's supremacy—as constitutionally exercised, that is—would be unacceptable. He did not theoretically rule out the use of force to bring protesting colonists back into line. But as late as 1774 he did not think the colonists had exceeded their rights or that force was required. In fact, he was even willing to deal with the Continental

Congress, which had absolutely no standing under the law as his parliamentary colleagues understood it. Although Congress at its inception was extra-legal rather than illegal because it broke no specific law by its existence, for the vast majority of men in parliament—and their king—the calling of that Congress had verged on treason.

Edmund Burke disagreed. He sided with Rockingham rather than Chatham on the issue of parliament's authority to tax the colonists and he was much more reluctant than Chatham to endorse extra-legal action. But like Chatham he felt that British leaders were pushing the colonists needlessly. Policies aimed at raising revenue that could reduce colonial trade and increase colonial resentment ought to be avoided at all costs. As the debates on what became the Coercive Acts began, he warned that the majority of members were stirring up resentment, as they had in 1765 and 1767. The results would be even worse because American suspicions ran that much deeper. The colonists' questioning of parliamentary authority to tax, unless parliament desisted, would lead to a questioning of parliament's authority over the colonies in any form. Since the colonists had lived for generations virtually autonomous, a privilege that they now considered a right, it was too late to make the empire into something other than what they understood it to be.

Burke was unpersuasive even if prescient. The majority view was expressed in February 1769, when the Commons and the Lords issued a sharp rebuke of colonial protest. They would not tolerate any questioning of the Declaratory Act, which had been on the increase. Sending out resolutions from one assembly to another was uncalled for, an inappropriate use of power that confounded the good and loyal people of the empire. Disobedient colonists in Boston, not tyrannical government in London, had been the reason for sending soldiers among civilians. Their combining with other dissidents in "audacious Usurpations of the Powers of Government" had disturbed the public peace in the Bay Colony. And yet parliament stood by as half of the troops sent to Boston were withdrawn in less than a year and the rest after the "Massacre." Some colonists interpreted their withdrawal as an admission of failure, not proof that order, as London understood it, had been restored. Colonial resolutions seemed to be achieving their aim in organizing protest; parliamentary resolutions rang hollow by comparison. They may have inadvertently fed the colonial tendency to thwart imperial authority. But even the shedding of blood in 1775 would not automatically bring with it a clear hardline policy at Westminster.

Shadow Governments

The Continental Congress that met in Philadelphia from September to October 1774 in reaction to the Coercive Acts was hardly the first inter-colonial gathering of delegates. Meetings involving representatives from multiple colonies dated back to the previous century. There they attempted to resolve disputes over boundaries, trade, and Indian relations. The agreements they reached, when they reached them, were only as binding as local authorities were willing to enforce. Imperial authorities back in London did not take official notice, either to condemn or to endorse their actions.

What is now referred to as the Stamp Act Congress of October 1765 continued that tradition of inter-colonial collaboration, but with a greater sense of urgency and with a greater potential for imperial disruption. This gathering of the disaffected to address issues raised by Grenville's program had been the brainchild of leaders in the lower house of the Massachusetts General Court. In June the house speaker sent out a request to his counterparts in twelve other colonies to appoint delegates who would meet in New York that October. The invitation went to all of the original thirteen states of the future new nation, although no one involved at the time saw the foundation that they poured. Quebec and the Floridas had no representative legislature, so they were not included. Nova Scotia did but was considered too much a creature of imperial administration to involve. Jamaica and other West Indies islands that had assemblies were not invited either because they were too far away and too disconnected by interest and identity.

Ultimately, delegates from nine colonies would convene in New York. They met for nearly three weeks and passed a series of resolutions. To have come from a colony was not the same as officially representing it, even if chosen to attend by the lower house of the assembly. Of the twenty-seven men there, only the delegates from Connecticut and Rhode Island can be said to have been acting officially for the colony, with their governor's blessing. For the other seven delegations it was more nebulous. In some cases the delegates were chosen formally by their respective assemblies. In the case of New Jersey, members of the lower house acted informally, choosing delegates even though the assembly was not then in session. Some delegates went with their assembly's official and governor's unofficial endorsement. Others went without either gubernatorial endorsement or condemnation, their governors hoping to avoid confrontation with them or a lecture from London. In Virginia and Georgia the governors made it clear that they would not call a legislative session to choose delegates for any such gathering.

As an extra-legal gathering, the Stamp Act Congress was just one indicator that a revolutionary subconscious had developed long before future revolutionaries made a conscious choice to leave the empire. More telling than the meeting in New York was the state of mind that brought men there, a changing identity that continued to develop over the next decade. Their understanding of their rights as Englishmen and their place as legislators within the imperial system often put them at odds with royally appointed governors as well as policy makers back in London. The tendency to act outside official governmental channels only increased after the Stamp Act crisis and became a colony-wide phenomenon.

As a response to the Townshend program, in February 1768 the Massachusetts lower house passed resolutions asserting colonial rights. It accepted subordination to parliament while seeking to limit its authority, an increasingly common mix of conciliatory and threatening language. Members sent their resolutions as a circular letter to other colonial assemblies. Both Governor Bernard and Secretary of State Hillsborough demanded that they rescind it; instead, they reaffirmed it by an even larger margin. Bernard ended the session and refused to call a new one when word came that troops had been dispatched. The Boston town meeting called for a convention of delegates from of all the towns in the province to meet in Boston that September. Over two hundred men elected by the freemen of over one hundred towns came. They passed resolutions echoing those of the lower house and included rumblings about resisting the troops when they arrived. They did not; they went home and the troops landed without incident. Nonetheless, they had hurled a rhetorical gauntlet at the feet of imperial authorities, in both Boston and London.

Variations on what happened in the Bay Colony would occur elsewhere. Take, for example, the response of Virginia legislators in 1769 to their governor's expectation that they go home, their service as members of the House of Burgesses being done until he called them back. He had ended the legislative session to silence their criticism of imperial policy and prevent their passing any protest resolutions. Instead, they went down a Williamsburg street to the upstairs room of a local tavern, passed their resolutions, had them published, and in effect asked the reading public to choose between allegiance to them or to their governor. There was nothing explicitly illegal, nothing intentionally revolutionary, in asking that the choice be made. But in effect those Virginians had begun the formation of an alternative political allegiance.

Crowds that formed to protest imperial policies, destroying property or tarring and feathering individuals, are the most famous but most transitory example that something more troubling was afoot. Far more important in forming a new identity were resolutions passed by one colony's assembly that might be endorsed by another, or the arguments made by the author of a pamphlet or newspaper piece printed in one colony that circulated in another, or the formation of groups like the Sons of Liberty and their inter-colonial communication, or the information-sharing activities of committees of correspondence, on both town and colony level, or civic groups devoted to promoting local industry or banding together to boycott imported British goods. All swore allegiance to crown and empire but all insisted that protest and petition were their right. Only as these inter-colonial connections were being formed could the divisive forces that had alienated one colony from another, or one group within a colony from another, be overshadowed—

not eliminated, but for a time be made to appear less pressing than the need to join in a common cause.

The meeting of a Continental Congress in 1774, nine years after the Stamp Act Congress, is proof that colonial alienation continued to spread. The precipitating cause was the same: a spate of parliamentary legislation, in this instance the Coercive Acts, that concerned colonists condemned even more roundly than they had Grenville's program. As in 1765 their protests were not simply against individual pieces of legislation but also against what that legislation as a whole, in their minds, signified.

Calls for this Congress came spontaneously from individuals, towns, and colonies before the first of the Coercive Acts—that closing the port of Boston—took effect. In 1774 colonial protestors ventured even further into the political gray area of extra-legal action than they had in 1765. Once again the Connecticut and Rhode Island delegations could be said to officially represent their colonies. The Pennsylvania legislature acted officially, though without waiting for the governor's approval. The Massachusetts lower house acted before General Thomas Gage, the recently arrived new governor, could end the session. Delegates from the other eight colonies—Georgia alone of the eventual thirteen to rebel sent no one—came by moving outside legitimate governmental channels. When members of Virginia's House of Burgesses attempted to choose delegates, their governor ended the session. They reconvened extra-legally as a provincial convention and made their selection. In other colonies there was true proto-revolutionary action, as towns and counties, most acting in concert with newly formed provincial conventions, chose delegates—meaning that the gathering in Philadelphia had even less legitimacy, in the eyes of Whitehall and Westminster, than the earlier meeting in New York.

With repeal of the Stamp Act in 1766, it had appeared to those hoping for a restoration of imperial harmony that the extra-legal action of disaffected colonial leaders was temporary, a product of the moment. Actually it was not. Protests against one program or another were not merely an example of transatlantic physics, each imperial action producing an equal and opposite colonial reaction. British irritation and colonial agitation grew in response to a multitude of issues, not just acts of parliament. The royal prerogative, whether exercised infrequently from Whitehall or more often through crown-appointed governors, proved equally as controversial. There was no simple ebb and flow, marked by each successive legislative enactment, from Grenville's to Townshend's to North's. Rather, the disputes generated by the actions taken in each ministry accentuated disagreements that were more fundamental and not necessarily tied to a specific policy. Those tensions were caused by the ill-defined nature of the imperial-colonial relationship and in that sense endemic rather than episodic.

As historian Jack P. Greene has emphasized, defenders of empire and champions of colonial rights talked past each other. Frustrated colonists pressed imperial authorities to recognize in theory what they already allowed in practice: a political autonomy that, in their eyes, validated what they claimed were fundamental rights that crown and parliament viewed as revocable privileges. Generally speaking, those who defended colonial American rights contended that they came from God through nature, as embodied in England's unwritten constitution and captured in positive law, including their charters. Political logic said that sovereignty had to be indivisible. Imperial reality defied that logic with an informal federalism, a division of power between imperial core and colonial periphery that reflected real conditions, not theoretical constructs. The masters of empire had neither the inclination nor wherewithal to impose their will on unwilling colonists. To some degree, Professor Greene reminds us, their authority had to be "negotiated" if the empire were to hold together as it became ever more diverse and far-flung. Increasingly the colonists demanded some sort of concession to their view of how they fit within the larger picture.

Even so the delegates who gathered at Philadelphia in September 1774, like their predecessors in New York nine years earlier, knew not to dredge up every possible grievance. They limited their complaints to postwar policies so that British leaders would date American discontent from 1763. They offered a point at which, in effect, the good empire went bad—postwar policies as talking point, with the restoration of mutual respect as a shared objective. In doing so they uneasily coupled principled response with pragmatic concern. After all, the professed purpose of their assembling was to persuade Whitehall and Westminster to chart a different, more conciliatory course, not react with harsher measures still.

In their resolutions and messages to the crown and both houses of parliament, the delegates to the 1765 congress had pledged their allegiance to the empire and attempted to reassure the king that they were his loyal subjects. They entreated rather than demanded and yet they added an essential qualification to their willingness to obey; namely, that they owed all "due subordination" to parliament. In their view that excluded direct taxation. They stressed that they were not and, as a practical matter, could not be adequately represented at Westminster. Therefore, by right, they should tax themselves through their own legislatures. Crown and parliament did not concede their point. Undeterred, colonial protestors would add that they only owed "due allegiance" to the crown as well.

Delegates to the 1774 Congress echoed their predecessors in some respects, and went beyond them in others. Given the heightened sense of crisis, they would consequently petition as more insistent supplicants. They all had been sent to Philadelphia with a charge to restore peace and harmony, which meant making their rights and their expectations for improved policies clear to Whitehall and Westminster. Professing loyalty to crown and empire, they pressed for new policies more sympathetic to their needs, more sensitive to their rights. On that general level the delegates could agree fairly easily. Settling on particulars would be more difficult. Patrick Henry proclaimed "I am not a Virginian, but an American," which other delegates understood was oratorical hyperbole mixed with a real political message to them all: if they could not unite, they could expect no change. Even so, Henry could not have been surprised that voting would be done by delegation, individual delegates only acting within that arrangement. It was an arrangement that would be kept the next time they met, an arrangement carried into the new national government formed in 1776.

Samuel Adams and others were convinced that the delegates needed to pass an American "bill of rights" to counter-balance parliament's 1766 Declaratory Act. In 1765 the Stamp Act Congress delegates had argued for their rights on the basis of the English Constitution, with God and natural rights left in the background. As in 1765, when making their case the 1774 delegates had to choose what to write and what to leave unwritten, when to be direct and when to be ambiguous. After much debate they decided to make the natural rights argument explicit, interwoven with the principles of the English Constitution and express guarantees included in their charters. They denied parliament's authority to tax them directly or to pass any legislation designed to raise revenue from them. They expressed a willingness to allow their trade to be regulated for the greater good of the empire, but whatever revenue was generated through that regulation had to be incidental rather than intentional. The colonists themselves would judge whether the distinction had been upheld. Moreover, they endorsed a view, asserted by protesting Bay colonists, that George III reigned as their king by compact, not hereditary right. They owed him fealty only if he honored the terms of that compact. In other words, they acted as king makers, having reached the point that both Franklin and Burke warned they would if they felt their demands had not been met.

Before adjourning with a vow to reconvene if crown and parliament did not respond satisfactorily, they called for the formation of the Continental Association. It followed what had been done informally by individuals, towns, and assemblies going back to the Stamp Act crisis. The association banned all trade with Britain, imports as well as exports, until the Coercive Acts were repealed. This was the most direct call yet for colonists to make a choice of political allegiance. Those not honoring the ban were to be harried by their neighbors, coerced unofficially into compliance through physical threat and moral suasion as well as officially through supporting legislation passed by the provincial conventions then taking form in most all of the colonies that rebelled the next year. To combat parliament Congress had emulated parliament, using its own carrot and stick approach to get what it wanted. Congress declared economic warfare ideally to head off military confrontation. In reality it helped make confrontation more likely.

Reform Rejected

Some of the delegates to the first Continental Congress left Philadelphia cautiously optimistic. They thought that there was a chance Whitehall and Westminster would overlook their extra-legal action and respond to their plea for an imperial softening. Joseph Galloway, delegate from Pennsylvania and onetime political ally of Benjamin Franklin, was not among them. He left convinced that the breach would only open wider—because of their efforts, not despite them. He had offered what he thought was an institutional solution to the problem of imperial administration: a permanent inter-colonial congress presided over indirectly by the king and sanctioned by parliament—indeed, not only sanctioned by parliament but a subordinate, component part of it. Individual colonies would keep their "present constitution" and regulate their internal affairs.

Galloway had come very close to winning approval, but once his motion was defeated, his proposal was not even included in the record of proceedings that the delegates shared with the public. Galloway's proposal had been inspired by Benjamin Franklin's Albany Plan, drafted in 1754 on the eve of the French and Indian War. The structure and intended purview were the same: delegates from individual colonies, chosen by their assemblies, would meet in a "Grand Council" to manage concerns over trade, land, and Indian policy. Whatever legislation they passed would be reviewed first by the royally appointed president general. If he approved, then it would be passed along to the king-in-council, who in turn would have three years to allow or disallow the Act—as with legislation coming out of individual colonies. Franklin's plan, although endorsed by his fellow delegates, was not acted on in London and the individual colonies either rejected or ignored it. That Franklin's proposal suffered such a fate on the eve of a war where the need for transatlantic and inter-colonial collaboration had been obvious did not augur well for Galloway's proposal twenty years later, when Anglo-American relations were far more strained.

The Franklin and Galloway plans are just the most famous of numerous proposals offered over the years to improve Anglo-American relations. Some, like those two, advocated an inter-colonial congress. Others suggested giving Americans seats in the British parliament. Still others suggested giving the individual colonies legislative autonomy, with the only tie between mother country and colonies to be through the king-in-council. Franklin himself at one time or another entertained all three possibilities and even briefly toyed with the idea of a new imperial parliament, beyond what already existed at Westminster.

Even imperial administrators frustrated by colonial protests could concede that the empire's foundation needed repair. In the aftermath of the Stamp Act disturbances in Boston during the summer of 1765, Francis Bernard, the royally appointed governor of Massachusetts, pressed London to alter the political relationship between mother country and colonies. Until that was done nothing but trouble lay ahead. He was convinced that the contest over the Stamp Act was, on a deeper level, a battle over parliamentary supremacy, with implications for Britain's sovereignty. "It is my opinion," he wrote to London, "that all the Political Evils in America" arose from the failure to define the proper formal relationship between mother country and colonies. Bernard felt so harried by 1768 that he did everything he could to get troops sent to Boston, but without asking in so many words. He would be all but driven from office the next year by his political opponents in the province, for that and other offenses that they accused him of committing.

It is true that he wanted colonial political autonomy curtailed and the Massachusetts Government Act of 1774 incorporated some of the recommendations that he had been making for nearly a decade. But he also wanted that governmental tightening to be accompanied with an economic loosening. So long as the navigation system attempted to close out trade with foreigners and restrict colonial manufacturing it was doomed to fail, he warned. Parliament should pass lower duties where possible, allow trade with foreigners not directly in competition with Anglo-American interests, and offer financial incentives to encourage the colonists to diversify. Bay colonists smuggled in lemons and wine from Portugal, laws to the contrary notwithstanding. Imperial administrators knew about such behavior but did nothing to stop it. For Bernard, the need to revamp a system and not pass laws that no one intended to obey or enforce was obvious.

Others who have come down to us as ideological hardliners were actually pragmatists, willing to do whatever it took to make the empire succeed. George Grenville, for one, did not object to the idea of seating Americans in parliament. He was not willing, however, to openly suggest that as a solution to the problem of representation because he was certain he would not be supported by his colleagues. By contrast, Quaker and London merchant Thomas Crowley spent over a decade trying to get Westminster interested in the idea of creating American seats—and also bringing in the Irish, to the Lords as well as the Commons. Both Ireland and the colonies would keep their existing legislative bodies to handle local affairs. Parliament would do double duty as a direct representative body for Britain and as the legislature for the larger empire. Crowley suggested eighty new seats in the Commons—fifty for the Americans, thirty for the Irish—and twenty new peers in the Lords, ten Irish and ten American. He could not interest anyone in his proposal, Benjamin Franklin included, despite his persistent lobbying.

Implicit in any plan to seat Americans at Westminster was this question: how many of them would it take for their voice to be effectively heard and for them to have a hand in shaping imperial policy? In September 1774, when the last parliamentary elections were held before the outbreak of fighting in the colonies, the House of Commons had seats for 558 members representing constituencies in England, Scotland, and Wales. There were just over 200 peers in the House of Lords. Those peers were divided between lords spiritual and temporal, the former composed of the two archbishops and twenty-four bishops, and the latter of the five ranks in the secular peerage: duke, marquess, earl, viscount, and baron. Rockingham was the only marquess; Hillsborough was the most recent earl, advanced by the king in part for his service as secretary of state for the American colonies. Members of Commons represented over three hundred constituencies in a combination of county and borough seats. Generally speaking, English constituencies were represented by two members, and those from Scotland and Wales, just one.

Treating an American province as the equivalent of an English county posed one set of problems; carving out American boroughs posed yet another. The idea of an American peerage would probably have stirred as much unrest in the colonies as resistance in Britain. George III, with the sole power to create new peerages, showed no inclination to do so across the Atlantic anyway. Baronets, who outnumbered members of the Commons and peers combined, did not hold seats in parliament but were a vital part of Britain's ruling class. They had been since the first baronetcies were created during the reign of James I. But creating baronets, who were commoners with hereditary titles, could have caused as much transatlantic controversy as naming American peers. Both houses of parliament were built around a distinctive social hierarchy, keeping England the most powerful element within Great Britain, and certain groups within England remained ascendant. In short, Britain's leaders and electorate differed substantially from those in the colonies, who had developed their own political culture.

Borough seats in the Commons, unlike those in colonial American assemblies, were not based on voter constituencies in the popular sense. The more modern concept captured in the phrase "one man-one vote" did not yet exist, in either the colonies or Britain. Defenders of the empire contended that the colonists, like all Britons, enjoyed "virtual" if not "actual" representation at Westminster. That is to say, members of parliament ostensibly thought broadly enough that they represented the entire empire, regardless of what particular seat they held. Although colonists argued against the notion of virtual representation that Grenville used in response to their demands, that did not make them eighteenth-century populists. Even though they denied that virtual representation at Westminster included them, they could accept that it applied to Britons. Their own legislators thought similarly about their relationship to the inhabitants in their own colonies.

John Cartwright, an Englishman whose proposal for imperial reform came on the eve of war, hoped to escape the controversies over representation raised by parliament versus provincial legislatures. Cartwright would become famous as an advocate of political reform within Britain. It is interesting that his reformist zeal first took him to consider the empire before he turned to the mother country. He agreed with Josiah Tucker that the imperial system was not working and could no longer be sustained. Unlike Tucker, he did not believe that the American colonies ought to be cut loose from the empire. Even though he dismissed the idea of American representation at Westminster in any form—virtual or actual—as "the wildest of all chimeras," he thought that an "American league" could still be formed within a "British Confederacy."

For Cartwright, social justice trumped legal nicety. Ultimately, he believed, the people were sovereign and all legitimate government was based on their consent. The only meaningful test of empire was if it secured the rights of its people. Faith in Britain's empire of liberty needed to be restored if the Anglo-American tie were to survive. Rome fell because it failed to remain true to higher principles. Britain need not suffer the same fate. But British America could only succeed if Americans wanted to remain part of the empire. They were entitled to use their inherent right to choose.

Chatham's failed last ditch effort in January 1775 to head off a confrontation by urging that Whitehall and Westminster deal with the Continental Congress rather than ignore it prompted Cartwright to add more details to his proposal. He guessed correctly that North's counter-proposal to Chatham, moving that parliament allow the colonies to meet requisition requirements that it set, with the issue of its ultimate authority unaddressed, would not be appealing to protesting Americans. That North also pressed for a provision restricting New England's trade until the colonies there fell back into compliance with imperial authority seemed to contradict what he claimed were conciliatory aims.

Under Cartwright's plan, crown, parliament, and commissioners from each of the colonies would work together to negotiate an arrangement agreeable to all. That new arrangement would not only protect the colonies already in existence, but also secure the future of new colonies created on the North American mainland. The primary tie to the empire would be through the crown. Parliament would renounce any claim to authority over the colonists. Whether or not Cartwright consciously echoed Franklin, he suggested that the other tie be through an inter-colonial congress presided over by a crown-appointed "ambassador general." Cartwright included a detailed map showing the projected boundaries and names of nineteen new colonies in the West, all the way to the Mississippi and curving back around north of the Great Lakes to Quebec. Cartwright even provided a population-based process by which the new colonies could be politically organized to join the others in their inter-colonial congress. He referred to the colonies as states or nations to underscore that British America would be a partner with Britain, in a transatlantic example of federalized power sharing. Interestingly enough, John Adams and Benjamin Franklin, independently of each other as well as of Cartwright, had come to see the empire as composed of multiple states united through the crown. Adams went so far as to wonder if the word "empire" even fitted what existed at all.

No one in parliament took up Cartwright's cause. Even if Cartwright's proposal had arrived in the colonies before the shooting started, it is not likely to have been championed by anyone there either. Benjamin Franklin, for his part, took one last stab at structural reform to end political impasse in July 1775. By then he had returned to Philadelphia from his many years in London as a lobbyist. A member of the second Continental Congress that convened in May, he drafted his plan after the fighting had begun in Massachusetts, neighboring New England colonies had rallied in support, and Congress had appointed George Washington as commander-in-chief of a new inter-colonial army. The New England war had thereby expanded to include any colonies willing to join in common cause.

Franklin understood that like-minded patriots, by moving from protest to revolt, were approaching a political impasse. He also understood that very few colonists anywhere, Massachusetts included, were publicly pressing for revolution. Congress, notably, did not characterize itself as the national government of an independent nation in the making.

The "Articles of Confederation and Perpetual Union," which Franklin described as a "firm league of friendship," captured his ambivalence and that of his colleagues in Congress. All of the colonies in British America would be invited to join. In an initial draft, Franklin even included Ireland. Those in support could act through their duly constituted assemblies or, in colonies where the extra-legal had effectively become the legal, through their provincial conventions. They would keep as much of their autonomy as they chose. They would send delegates to an inter-colonial congress that would do everything necessary to provide for the "general welfare" of them all, including raising troops and taxes by requisition. If the king responded favorably to the petition sent to him by the first Continental Congress and parliament repealed the legislation that had provoked "this unjust war" against American rights, then peace could be restored. "On the arrival of these events the Colonies will return to their former Connection and Friendship," Franklin promised, before ending with this threat: "but on failure thereof this Confederation will be perpetual." And with that Franklin made the implicit possibility of revolution explicit.

Toward Independence

Franklin's fellow delegates discussed his proposal but they did not approve it. There was consequently no point in passing it along to Whitehall or Westminster. It would soon be relegated to the same figurative dustbin as every other reform proposal that had come along in these years, on either side of the Atlantic. It is somehow fitting that Franklin was there through it all, from Albany in 1754 to Philadelphia in 1775. During the London years in between, he had once lamented that he seemed to fall between cultural stools: not quite British enough in British eyes to be truly welcomed there; not quite American enough from the colonists' perspective to be trusted to protect their interests. But we should not jump to the conclusion that a hyphenated identity was impossible to sustain in the empire. Thirteen American colonies rose in rebellion; even more stayed loyal. All had issues with the nature of imperial authority and the distribution of power within the empire. But not all saw separation as preferable, including many thousands who lived in the colonies that did fight to leave.

During the February 1766 debates in the House of Lords over repeal of the Stamp Act, the Earl of Mansfield, chief justice of the Court of King's Bench, showed that Benjamin Franklin had not been alone in his dire warnings of that moment. Mansfield rejected the various arguments that the colonists were making about how parliament had violated their rights. He singled out James Otis's 1764 pamphlet for particular scorn. Otis, a Massachusetts lawyer and rising leader in Boston politics, had used a natural rights foundation in making the colonists' case. He also contended that the only solution to the problem of parliament legislating for the colonies was to give Americans seats in it. Mansfield knew that many of his colleagues dismissed Otis's arguments as outlandish, his pamphlet as unworthy of notice. "It may be called silly and mad," Mansfield admitted, but, he also cautioned, those with mad or silly ideas "have led the people to rebellion, and overturned empires."

What appeared to Mansfield as ungrateful colonists making unreasonable demands was, from some colonists' perspective, loyal subjects driven to desperation by an oppressive parliament and a king who failed to intercede when they called on him for help. In 1766 most protesting colonists were still limiting their criticism of the empire to acts of parliament rather than condemning parliament itself. The king they criticized obliquely if at all.

Demands unmet, over the next decade they would reject parliament's authority altogether and blame the king for their troubles. The inflammatory language of Thomas Paine's *Common Sense* tilled political soil that would be planted by Thomas Jefferson in his declaration of independence and then harvested by the Continental Congress when it edited Jefferson's text, adopted it, and sent it out to the newly proclaimed American nation, and to the world beyond. What we need to appreciate is how that 1776 declaration, the culmination of what began as an attempt to secure rights in the empire, became the basis for something quite different. In their quest, as Paine put it, "to begin the world over again," American Revolutionaries combined three elements equally important to them: an independent nation, republican in principle, and federal in form.

Part II

World War

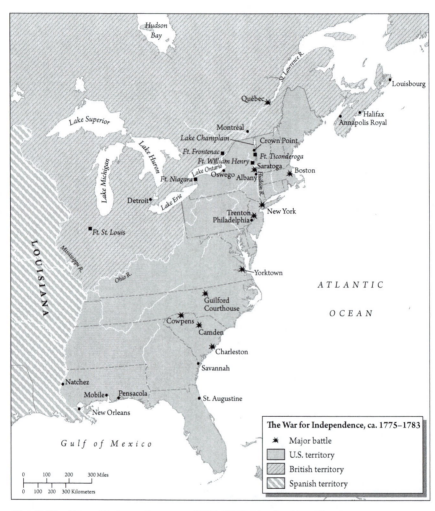

Map 2 The War of Independence, ca. 1775–1783. Map by Alice Thiede,
CARTO-GRAPHICS

Chapter 4

Rebellion Becomes Revolution

Provincial Power over Imperial Authority

One of the more familiar tales coming out of the War of American Independence is how a column of British soldiers who ventured into the Massachusetts countryside in April 1775 almost did not make it back to Boston alive. What is sometimes forgotten is what took the redcoats out of Boston in the first place. General Thomas Gage sent them forth because, as governor of Massachusetts, his authority was not recognized in the province, except where his soldiers or the Royal Navy could make a show of force. He had arrived to replace Thomas Hutchinson in the spring of 1774. By the summer he deduced that, politically, he was beaten, as Hutchinson had been before him. Boston, troop-free since the aftermath of the 1770 "Massacre," once again had British soldiers on its streets. They were stationed among colonial civilians and yet, once again, they did not act as an army of occupation nor were town officials displaced by martial law. The political half-measures and half-hearted enforcement of imperial policies had not ended.

Gage could not implement the provisions of the Massachusetts Government Act in the face of local opposition. His impossible task, he learned through repeated frustration, was to restore imperial authority, to retake what had long been lost—ideally without shedding any blood. We can get an idea of the obstacles he faced by noting what happened to the governor's council that was supposed to take office under the new Act. Thirty-six names appeared on Gage's list of royally approved appointees. Eleven declined to take the oath of office. Of the twenty-five who did agree to serve, nine soon after resigned.

The sixteen who remained were all subjected to the sort of community pressure visited upon council member John Murray of Rutland, a small town to the west of Boston. A crowd of over one thousand men, including local militia officers, assembled outside his house. They brought muskets but stacked them out of sight. A few demanded the right to search the house for Murray. Not finding him—forewarned, he had fled to Boston—they told his family that unless he resigned his seat he could expect another, even less friendly visit. He did not resign nor did he return. He remained in Boston and, with his family, sailed away when the British evacuated Boston in March 1776. They found a new home in Nova Scotia. Their old home, with the other property they abandoned in Rutland, was confiscated by the state and later sold at public auction. It was typical of what happened to thousands of other loyalists throughout the colonies.

In June, Gage had ended the General Court's legislative session, but with the understanding that he would call for elections to prepare for a new session in October. He did not call for the election and he did not schedule a new session. In response, town and county leaders throughout the colony elected delegates to represent them in a provincial convention. In between there were hundreds of locally instituted actions like that directed at John Murray. To the west, in Berkshire and Hampshire counties, large crowds composed of leading men as well as common folk had assembled to prevent court sessions from being conducted under the provisions of the Massachusetts Government Act. By October, Massachusetts had not one government but two, each vying for the people's allegiance. A similar scene would be played out elsewhere over the next twelve months, from Georgia to New Hampshire. Connecticut and Rhode Island were almost alone in being spared the trauma of disruptive political change.

Initially Gage had dismissed those unwilling to stand alongside him in defense of imperial authority as timid, even cowardly. With time he better understood that his opponents were more than just a few "demagogues" and that a new body politic, with new loyalties, was forming. "Civil government is near its end," he lamented after six months in the Bay Colony. "Nothing can be done except by forcible means," he complained in exasperation. "A check anywhere could be fatal and the first stroke will decide a great deal," he surmised. At least he got that much right.

Angered by reports of what was transpiring, the king had considered the New England colonies to be in a state of rebellion as early as November 1774. What he expressed in private, parliament made public in February 1775 as it approved a New England trade ban. The king did not formally declare New England in rebellion until the following August, long after receiving word of the fighting at Lexington and Concord, but fairly soon after learning about the slaughter at Bunker Hill in June. As far as he, his ministers, and a clear majority in parliament were concerned, the Bay colonists resisting Gage's authority had been verging on treason since the Tea Party. Creating their own alternative governmental forms topped the list of their treasonable acts. Working through the provincial convention, with the cooperation of local officials, self-proclaimed Massachusetts patriots had expropriated the king's taxes for their own purposes. That included equipping and training a reconstituted militia. This new militia, purged of those politically out of step, promised to defend the people's liberties and to not disband until satisfied that crown and parliament had seen the error of their ways. Town companies were organized into regiments in what, for the moment, was a paper provincial army under a nominal commanding general. Gage's opponents had gone so far as to claim that they defended the fundamental rights that he violated and that therefore he and those Bay colonists who supported him were the real traitors. Needless to say, none of this, in the king's view, could be justified.

Massachusetts patriots saw things differently then, as do their present-day descendants. Lexington and Concord continue to vie for credit as the site of the true first shot of the American Revolution. Local pride is understandable but the choices of July 1776 should not be read back into the actions of April 1775. The Massachusetts militiamen who turned out on April 19—well over three thousand of them from perhaps forty neighboring towns—did not take up arms as rebels, much less revolutionaries. In their minds they fought for hearth and home as descendants of transplanted Englishmen, good and true. Many had the unrealistic expectation that perhaps their king would side with them against the evil ministers who had led Britain astray, and the illegitimate government that Gage headed. What finally exploded that April morning could have happened a number of times before: in the previous September, with the so-called "powder alarm" in Cambridge, or the following February, when a British force nearly got itself into what would have been a disastrous skirmish at Salem.

Parliament passed a second Act cutting off trade with additional colonies not long after it banned trade with New England. In effect, parliament on one side, the Continental Congress and provincial conventions on the other, were exchanging unspoken declarations of war. They used the marketplace as a proxy battlefield. From Whitehall and Westminster's perspective, disloyal colonists had acted first and they had had no choice but to retaliate. Both used the rhetoric of just war, claiming that they acted defensively. Congress characterized the Boston Port Act as proof of parliament's warlike intentions. Parliament condemned in similar manner the Continental Association. Since the definitions of just war then prevailing under international law allowed for interpreting legislative enactments and civil disobedience as forms of war, rival disputants in a political contest could claim that they had been attacked even if a shot had not been fired. That is precisely what Congress and parliament did before events at Lexington and Concord.

Parliament included Virginia in the second trade ban because it had seemingly become all too much like Massachusetts. It too had fallen under the sway of protestors who professed loyalty to the crown and empire even as they denounced acts of parliament and moved outside duly constituted authority to seize political control. With a larger, more diverse population than the Bay Colony, imperial authorities were more surprised by the outbreak there. Dissident elements came together to organize a provincial convention even before their counterparts to the north. Leading members of the House of Burgesses repeated in 1774 what they had done in 1769. As before, the governor ended their legislative session to prevent their acting in concert with other protestors, this time against the pending Coercive Acts. Most of the Burgesses reconvened in the Raleigh Tavern and called for the provincial convention that assembled in Williamsburg that August and elected delegates to the First Continental Congress. The men who attended had been chosen by county conventions that passed resolutions echoing each other in condemning imperial policy as they asserted colonial rights. Not every county participated nor did all of the electors in those that did. Nonetheless, the dissidents professed to represent the whole colony, a claim contested there and elsewhere, but a claim that could stand as long as the initiative remained with the dissidents—as it would in Virginia and ultimately in all thirteen of the colonies who rebelled.

Virginians in the spring of 1775 did not have a confrontation to match that of Lexington and Concord. They did have a close call, in their version of the Massachusetts powder alarm the previous September. Fearing that the disloyal might seize munitions stored in Williamsburg, Governor Dunmore had them removed by a detail of Royal Navy sailors. Dunmore's opponents claimed that he had unlawfully seized property belonging to the people of the province. Dunmore countered that it belonged to the king and he performed lawfully as the king's deputy. He acted before receiving word of what had occurred in Massachusetts. His opponents grew in number when that news arrived, just days later. Local militia units that had gathered already were joined by others and threatened violence. Calmer heads prevailed and they dispersed, but tensions remained. Dunmore called the House of Burgesses back into session in June but soon after fled Williamsburg and took refuge on a British warship. Suspicion turned to enmity, royal government essentially came to an end and Virginia became self-governing—but without considering itself on the road to revolution and independence. The provincial convention reconvened in July. It filled the power vacuum and endorsed what the second Continental Congress had resolved to do the month before. But even as late as August 1775, convention delegates pledged their allegiance to George III and promised to disband "whenever our dangers are removed."

The Continental Congress reconvened on 10 May, 1775, as delegates had decided the previous October if Whitehall and Westminster did not respond to their resolutions—which neither had. Delegates still professed to want reconciliation even as they adopted the war in Massachusetts as their own. By then Gage's army, though reinforced, was clearly under siege. The Massachusetts provincial convention had appealed to neighboring colonies for help. They responded and Boston with its eight thousand or so British troops was ringed by perhaps fifteen thousand militiamen, mostly from Massachusetts, but with contingents from New Hampshire as well as

Connecticut and Rhode Island. It was a demonstration of regional unity that many in London twenty years before never would have predicted. After the bloody fighting on June 17 on Breed's and Bunker hills, where British regulars, at great loss, drove New England militiamen off the Charlestown peninsula and thereby secured their flank, both sides had gone into general inactivity. The British were too few to break out; the militiamen, lacking large-bore artillery, could not drive the soldiers from Boston or Royal Navy warships from the harbor.

Massachusetts had also appealed to Congress for aid. Congress responded in the middle of June. First, it authorized rifle companies from Pennsylvania, Maryland, and Virginia to be recruited for service in the Bay Colony. Well over a thousand volunteers answered the call. They proved to be a mixed bag; expert marksmen, perhaps, but ill suited for siege tactics. Next, Congress appointed George Washington, one of its members, as commander-in-chief of the newly constituted Army of the United Colonies. Washington had military experience, he was from Virginia, and he could be expected to serve as Congress directed, accepting that military leaders needed to defer to civilian authority. Congress then selected a mix of men from different colonies to act as major generals and brigadier generals to flesh out the army's command structure. Charles Lee, a retired British army officer living in Virginia, was the most experienced of the four major generals. He became proof that experience and wisdom are not always paired. He had fought in the French and Indian War, but then so had the other three major generals: Israel Putnam of Connecticut, Philip Schuyler of New York, and Artemas Ward of Massachusetts. Ward had been commander of the Massachusetts troops under the provincial convention, then the larger New England army organized under the Bay Colony's leadership. He accepted his subordination to Washington with good grace, as had Massachusetts to Congress. Circumstances left no other realistic choice.

Thoughts of forming a true national army, with men from all of the colonies mixed together in the same regiments, had to be abandoned as the fighting expanded. When the Continental Army was formally constituted after the Declaration of Independence, troops were brigaded and paid by state. Militia companies kept their distinct local identities even as they were brought under the command structure created by Congress—so too state regiments that drew on the militia. In a sense, then, there was a federally based American military before there was an American nation. Historian Don Higginbotham argued persuasively that it is hard to imagine the United States taking the shape it did without the fighting that called it into existence. As a nation born in war it had to be something more than a loose confederacy. Shared political frustrations, or a shared vision apart from that struggle, would not have been enough to serve as a national foundation.

The New Nation

George Washington arrived in Cambridge to assume command early in July. It would take him until the following March to finally achieve his objective of liberating Boston. For most of the time in between it was as if he led American Lilliputians against the British Gulliver. Eventually he was able to place artillery pieces on Dorchester heights, overlooking Boston. Those cannons had been captured at Fort Ticonderoga the previous May; it took many months to haul them overland from New York. General William Howe, who had replaced Gage, canceled his planned attack on the American position and reached an agreement with Washington allowing him to evacuate. He and his troops, accompanied by well over one thousand loyalists, took a month to evacuate and sail north out of Boston harbor to Halifax. Many of those loyalists would never return. They lost the property they left behind, sold at public auction once they were condemned in absentia. But none of that could happen until Massachusetts reconstituted itself as a new state in a new nation, making the civil war—in the eyes of patriots, anyway—a conflict between sovereign powers. For their part, the British did not see the evacuation of Boston as anything more than an operational necessity.

In the meantime Washington learned the difficulties of commanding citizen soldiers and of turning amateurs into professionals. The frustrations that he felt as a Virginian dealing with New Englanders who typically elected their militia officers on the company level were only compounded by his inability, before March 1776, to force the issue with the British. Then there were the difficulties he faced with securing provisions for an army to keep it in the field. Those problems would vex him for the entire eight years that he served as commander-in-chief. As Washington prepared to shift his forces south to New York, where he could anticipate that the British would choose as their point of return, he knew that Congress's attempt to expand the political movement north into Canada was not going well.

Congress authorized a northern military campaign not long after it sent Washington to Massachusetts, in the vain hope that Canadians would join the revolt. Most French Canadians and even some recent Anglo-American transplants preferred neutrality to taking sides, and as many chose to defend the empire as rise against it. A two-pronged assault had converged on Quebec by December. The invading force moving up the Lake Champlain corridor under General Richard Montgomery had done well enough to take Montreal before advancing toward Quebec. The other contingent moved up the Kennebec River in Maine under Colonel Benedict Arnold. Stumbling through the woods for weeks before reaching the south bank of the St. Lawrence, Arnold's men were in sad shape once they rendezvoused with Montgomery. They combined to attack on the night of December 30. Montgomery and Arnold needed to act by then before losing men whose enlistments expired the next day. They failed miserably. Montgomery was killed and Arnold wounded. The survivors camped outside the city walls through the winter, with scant reinforcement. It would be too generous to say that they were truly laying siege. With spring and the arrival of British reinforcements they began a long retreat that carried them all the way down into New York by the fall. They would never be back.

Even as Congress raised an army and went to war, it attempted to justify itself to disconcerted Britons and unconvinced colonists. In declaring the "causes and necessities" of resistance, it blamed parliament for what had happened: parliament had attempted to enslave the colonists; they had resisted in self-defense. Having helped Britain defeat France, their common foe, they had been rewarded with abusive policies, with their rights trampled, their needs ignored, and their innocent blood shed. "Our cause is just. Our union is perfect," Congress proclaimed. Americans were determined to die "Free-men rather than to live Slaves." But they coupled threat with plea, their growing resentment with residual sentiment. In a petition sent to George III composed at almost the same moment, it pled, in more conciliatory language, for relief from despair. Members of Congress still professed to be "faithful subjects" of their king. Wrongs could be made right because they sought a restoration of "peace and harmony" in the empire that had been their only home.

The king refused to receive their petition and denounced them as rebels. And yet it would take another fourteen months for the protestors who had turned to rebellion to embrace revolution. In retrospect we tend to see Paine's *Common Sense*, published in January 1776, as capturing the new— the proper—American state of mind, irresistible because inevitable. Paine stressed that a bad king was only superficially the problem; the real problem was monarchy itself. Therefore the only solution was for Americans to declare their independence, found their own nation, and base it on republican principles. "A government of our own is our natural right," Paine told his readers. They would need to eliminate all hereditary privilege, not just monarchy: there could be no American king, no American house of lords.

Both politically and socially Paine pushed past most of his fellow patriots. But he was a good enough social psychologist to understand that his utter condemnation of Britain's empire and monarchical government could only be made after blood had been shed. Arguments that he had wanted to make earlier he saved until after April 19, 1775, which for him marked the point of no return. The fighting at Lexington and Concord exposed the lie that the empire was somehow a family or even a community of interests. "The blood of the slain, the weeping voice of nature cries, 'Tis Time to Part," Paine insisted. But as John Adams had commented in July 1775, over two months after Congress reconvened, many of his colleagues continued to experience "strange oscillations." They veered between love and hate of Britain, vacillating between a desire for war and a longing for peace because they were unsure of their proper course. Choosing to embrace the extra-legal, whether serving in a provincial convention or in the Continental Congress, did not automatically turn one into a revolutionary. Those few like Paine who decided that the end had come once the shooting started would have to wait until subsequent events drove more reluctant patriots to that same conclusion.

Congressional delegates from North Carolina had been authorized to support a motion for independence by April 1776, but they could not make that motion themselves. Virginia delegates were authorized to do so in May, to the relief of New Englanders like John Adams who had bided their time, waiting for just such a development. By then Congress had already advised all of the provincial conventions and assemblies supporting the rebellion to reconstitute their governments. It was not specifically a call for them to declare their independence; rather, it was a recommendation that they do what was most "conducive to the happiness and safety of their constituents in particular, and America in general." No one in Congress thought that meant military surrender or political retreat.

When delegate Richard Henry Lee of Virginia moved (with a second by John Adams) that Congress pass a resolution declaring its independence, most members of Congress understood that to object vigorously would not have made much sense. Why were they there, if not to secure American rights, and how could they any longer hope to do so within the empire? Thus the sequence of events leading to a declaration of independence on July 2 and approval of the document two days later explaining what had compelled them to make that choice.

In declaring independence, Congress showed its desire to look ahead to the future more than back to the past. It deleted an explicit lamentation offered by Jefferson about leaving the empire and yet it left a hint of regret by conceding that Americans were choosing independence only after a "long train of abuses" drove them to it. Unlike Paine, Congress did not mock the notion of an English constitution that had guaranteed their rights. It did make clear that whatever had governed the past no longer applied. Now was time for Americans to take their rightful place as a "separate and equal nation to which the laws of Nature and of Nature's God" entitled them. Higher principles bracket specific complaints in the declaration, each connected to the other.

In seeking to make their case "to a candid world," they hoped to prove that Revolutionary Americans fought for something more than their own self-interest, that concerned individuals had banded together to defend the common good. The "candid world" included fellow Americans who wanted no part of the civil war that the revolutionaries had precipitated or of the nation they proclaimed now existed. To build their new community they had to start with a new identity. George III was now the target of their obloquy. They had looked to him for protection from parliamentary excess;

now they denounced him. By escalating arguments they had eventually made parliament irrelevant. Eighteen times, while enumerating twenty-seven particular grievances, they accused George III of tyrannical rule. To read the list is to review the Revolutionary American view of a king who had violated their trust and made the empire of liberty a sham. Placing petty restrictions on their trade, imposing vice-admiralty judges who undercut their own common-law courts, attempting to free royal appointees from popular oversight by creating a civil list, disallowing laws passed by their own legislatures, sabotaging charter rights, stationing soldiers among civilians—all proved his disregard for them. And once the fighting started he had "plundered our seas, ravaged our coasts, burnt our towns, and destroyed the lives of our people." By his own disgraceful conduct he was their king no more.

They did not include Paine's utter condemnation of monarchy. They said nothing of the federal forms that would define their new government. Their assertion that "all men are created equal" would prove problematical soon enough. Even though African Americans fought on both sides, their military service had little effect on prevailing racial attitudes. The failure of the Revolution's leaders to close the gap between the rhetoric of freedom and the practice of slavery would haunt the new nation. So would their dualistic characterization of the Americans as "one people" who nonetheless lived in "free and independent states." To them it was a founding document in a more limited sense than it would be for future generations.

At the same time that a committee had been formed to write a declaration of independence, two others had been put in place: one to write a constitution that would outline the governmental structure of their new union, and another to secure the foreign alliances upon which their new nation would depend for its survival. By then members of Congress were anticipating a great confrontation between their army and an expeditionary force sailing for New York to launch the biggest amphibious operation Great Britain had ever undertaken.

There and Back Again

Even as the first of Washington's troops arrived in the New York area, marching overland from Boston, Governor William Tryon remained in the colony. Having sought sanctuary on a Royal Navy warship off Staten Island, he kept up the illusion of imperial authority. But the colony was no longer his or the king's. In New York and elsewhere beyond New England, towns and counties had proceeded with elections, some in response to the Coercive Acts, others only after the fighting began. All of the royally appointed governors to the south of New York, from Virginia through the Carolinas to Georgia, had fled their posts. The proprietary colonies of Pennsylvania and Maryland had also undergone subtle political transformations. Provincial conventions in most of those colonies smoothed the way for reconstituted assemblies to consolidate power and represent themselves as the legitimate authority. Thirteen colonies were slipping away. From London's perspective, a military solution had to be applied to a political problem.

George Germain, secretary of state for the American colonies, was charged by the king with coordinating Britain's military strategy. He had wanted to get a relief expedition to the southern colonies before any of this could happen. He was too late. Putting together troops and a fleet took longer than he had anticipated, and by the time the expedition arrived in American waters, the patriots and their alternative governments had taken control. There had been some fighting before then between patriot and loyalist militias—at Great Bridge in Virginia and Moore's Creek Bridge in North Carolina, notably—but with few casualties and perhaps a thousand men on each side. The British moved down the coast and attempted to take Charleston in June. They were driven off and sailed north to join in the build-up for the New York campaign. With that the entire region, from the Chesapeake south through Georgia, fell under the undisputed control of the opposition forces. That control would remain all but unchallenged for well over three years.

Washington had several months to prepare for the combined British fleets, whose lead elements began filling New York harbor by the end of June. There would be over seventy warships and hundreds of troop and supply vessels. The massive ships-of-the-line no doubt inspired awe as they dropped anchor. Frigates and sloops plied Long Island Sound and the Hudson River at will because Washington had no navy to stop them. The transports eventually disgorged over thirty thousand regulars, a third of them Hessian mercenaries. Washington had twenty thousand men to oppose them, the largest number he would ever have directly under his field command. They were a hodgepodge of Continentals and militia, some well equipped and trained, but most not, and almost none battle tested.

The British concentrated their forces on Staten Island. From his headquarters in New York City, Washington scattered his men, trying to contain the British and anticipate where they would strike first. He posted troops to the west of Staten Island in New Jersey, with some in a "flying camp" as the ready reserve. Most were bivouacked around Manhattan or on Long Island. Fort Lee had been thrown up on the New Jersey shore, and Fort Washington opposite it on Manhattan, to prevent the British from sailing up the Hudson. That neither fort had the firepower to prevent ships from running past them was just one indication of the odds against the Americans.

On August 22 the British landed in force on Long Island. Five days later they swept all before them. Using a frontal feint with a flanking movement around the American defenses, the British easily drove their opponents from the field and into Brooklyn, with their backs against the East River. With too little too late, Washington had rushed over with reinforcements. The general was fortunate to escape at all, as he and his troops were ferried by small boats across the East River to Manhattan. Some of the Americans had fought bravely; some had fled in a panic. None could match their opponents in open or broken-field tactics, the superiority of professionals over amateurs being all too apparent.

Washington had two more narrow escapes ahead of him, the first off of Manhattan Island in September and the second near White Plains in October, which prompted his flight into New Jersey in November. Each time his troops proved too unpredictable, too erratic to rely upon—and his errors compounded the problems. With hindsight he no doubt regretted leaving the garrison of Fort Washington behind to hold its position as he withdrew the bulk of his army into New Jersey. The fort fell within a matter of hours, delivering well over two thousand prisoners into Howe's hands. Americans would not suffer such a loss of prisoners again until the surrender of Charleston in May 1780, when over four thousand were captured. Despite the fall of one fort, Washington abandoned the other (Fort Lee) most reluctantly as he began a retreat diagonally across New Jersey. He pressed on as quickly as his beaten, exhausted men could to stay ahead of the pursuing British. He thought that if he could cross the Delaware River into Pennsylvania the British would not venture after him that late into the campaign season.

The British did not pursue the rag-tag Americans very vigorously. Howe assumed that they could be mopped up the following spring. He knew that the eight thousand man army driving south from Canada under Guy Carleton would not make it to New York before year's end anyway. Advancing only part way down the Lake Champlain corridor, it withdrew and encamped above the lake. Carleton had no plans to renew the offensive until the following spring. The British occupied Newport, Rhode Island, in December. They could use Newport as a base of naval operations the next year, possibly cutting off Massachusetts ports by sea as New England could be isolated from New York along the Hudson River. Then the rebels who had started it all could be choked into submission. If they gave up, then presumably those elsewhere who had foolishly followed their lead would do the same.

Washington had left some of his troops behind in New York when he retreated across New Jersey, not knowing for certain whether Howe would press north or Carleton continue south. Once he was sure that neither was advancing, he brought some of those troops to him in Pennsylvania. Having started the campaign with twenty thousand, he was now down to fewer than six thousand under his immediate command and he would lose well over half of them with expiring enlistments at the end of December. Many of those no longer with him had drifted away, in their minds neither deserters nor traitors. Less than half had been lost to battlefield action as killed, wounded, or captured. Despite his army's reduced state, Washington became convinced that he could not simply go into winter quarters. He might not have an army left come spring and British pacification of New Jersey might succeed in the restoration of imperial authority. If he did not do something to reverse the trend, defeat could potentially lead to defeatism.

Thomas Paine had joined the retreating Americans as they traversed New Jersey and passed into Pennsylvania. "These are the times that try men's souls," he scribbled famously on a drumhead in camp. "The summer soldier and the sunshine patriot will, in this crisis, shrink, from the service of his country." Washington, Paine was confident, would not be one of the faint-hearted; he was made of sterner stuff. And, after what Washington accomplished over the next few weeks Paine would celebrate him as the American Fabius—a flattering analogy to the Roman general who, in the third century BC, had kept up the fight against invading Carthaginians overrunning Italy. A desperate Roman Senate had appointed Fabius dictator. Congress would not make Washington dictator but it did give him independent command as it fled an exposed Philadelphia for the greater safety of Baltimore.

Washington re-crossed the Delaware on Christmas night, a daring maneuver that succeeded because Washington finally enjoyed some luck that he coupled with improving skills. Three columns were supposed to cross the river; only Washington's of twenty-four hundred men made it across, hitting the Hessian outpost at Trenton. The Hessians were utterly surprised and surrendered after a brisk fight. Washington took them with him back into Pennsylvania and had the satisfaction of parading his nearly one thousand captives through the streets of Philadelphia—a first for the Americans.

Having gambled once successfully, Washington, up to full strength with perhaps five thousand men, decided to go again. He took his force back into New Jersey on December 30, thinking he could strike the British supply depot at Brunswick, another twenty miles ahead. But on his way there he almost ran into a relief column led by Charles, Earl Cornwallis, marching for Trenton, too late to relieve the Hessians. Washington knew that Cornwallis's men outnumbered and outclassed his own, so he reversed course and made a stand at Trenton that gave him a bit of breathing room. Then, winding his way along the shore of the Delaware River, he slipped past Cornwallis and won a brief but sharp skirmish at Princeton on January 3. He continued north with his little army to Morristown. There he went into winter quarters, sheltered in the low New Jersey hills. His counterattack caused Howe to pull most of his outposts back toward the eastern edge of New Jersey, disrupting pacification of the local population and enabling the Americans to forage for supplies and keep the Revolutionary cause alive in that state.

Washington learned as he went. As long as he could keep an army in the field, the British were losing and he was in some sense winning, though he had no grand major battlefield victories to his credit. At year's end Washington had shown a decisiveness, an audacity borne of desperation, that surprised his opponents and even some of his fellow patriots. Undeniably the war of attrition, even at this early stage, took a heavy toll on his men, with their constant shortages of virtually everything, from housing to food to clothing to guns and ammunition. The British suffered little by comparison, though they had expected crushing the rebellion to be so much easier than it was proving to be.

Quid Pro Quo?

Britain's big push of 1776 had been poorly coordinated and launched late in the campaign season. The 1777 campaign, despite many months of preparation, would be only slightly better planned and even more poorly coordinated. The strategic objectives that Germain laid out for 1777 were the same as those of 1776: send one column south down the Champlain corridor and another north along the Hudson. The Americans, obliged to prevent their joining, would be smashed to pieces in the ensuing battles. New England would be cut off and isolated, and the rebellion would then collapse.

Howe kept his position as overall commander, with field command of the army operating out of New York. General John Burgoyne replaced Guy Carleton as commander of the northern force. Howe had well over twenty thousand regulars, both British and Hessians. Burgoyne would have over ten thousand regulars, Brunswickers as well as British, and it was expected that he would have half again that number of Canadian and New York loyalist militia, with Indian allies to flesh out his forces.

In theory Howe and Burgoyne were to work in tandem. In reality they did not pull together at all. Germain allowed each general to go about achieving the larger objective his own way. Each promised to help the other, to be in place for their pincer movement at the decisive moment. Neither carried through and each bears the blame: Howe for not getting to Burgoyne in time, Burgoyne for pressing ahead even though he knew that Howe would not be there to assist him. Howe was convinced that he could take Philadelphia, the rebel capital, ninety miles to the southwest of New York City, and still have plenty of time to then link up with Burgoyne somewhere around Albany, one hundred and fifty miles up the Hudson. Burgoyne would have to fend for himself until Howe turned north and Germain did not insist on pinning down when that would be. Ultimately both of these professionals behaved most unprofessionally. By contrast, George Washington, who faced Howe, and General Horatio Gates, who ultimately faced Burgoyne, worked far more effectively to assist each other.

Howe and Burgoyne both fell victim to their own attempts at strategic cleverness. Howe thought that he might somehow trick Washington into a fight he could not win. Howe wasted months in pointless maneuvering.

Burgoyne decided to divide his army, the largest component to move directly down the Champlain corridor. A smaller column would deploy in a flanking movement from the west, along the Mohawk River from a starting point on the eastern shore of Lake Ontario. In retrospect it is hard to understand how this looked good to Burgoyne, even on a map.

The smaller force under Barry St. Leger never came close to linking up with Burgoyne. St. Leger had perhaps fifteen hundred men, a polyglot group of British regulars, Hessians, loyalist militia and Iroquois allies. That was not even half the size of the force as originally planned. Fort Stanwix, St. Leger's first major obstacle, stood one hundred miles to the west of Albany, in the Mohawk River Valley. It had a garrison of seven hundred or so New Yorkers. St. Leger lay siege to it and drove off a first attempt at relief, but then decided to withdraw rather than engage a second relief column led by Benedict Arnold. The fighting around Stanwix began in early August and was over before the end of the month. St. Leger pulled back and was not a factor in the later campaign, though he did try to rejoin the main column. Burgoyne knew about St. Leger's retreat soon enough but he was undeterred and pressed south.

Nor had he been deterred by the loss of a large foraging expedition that he sent into the Vermont country at about the same moment that St. Leger began his siege at Fort Stanwix. Local militiamen, joined by others from New Hampshire and Massachusetts, fell upon the thousand or so Brunswickers, Canadians, and Indians on August 16. Too far from Burgoyne to fight their way back to him or for him, if he had known their predicament, to cut his way through, they surrendered. Their fate showed that the unpredictability of the patriot militia worked both ways. Too often their quirks hurt American performance in battle; occasionally, as happened here at the Battle of Bennington, those very quirks had worked to the Americans' advantage.

Burgoyne had emerged from the woods south of the Champlain area at the end of July. When he finally reached the Hudson a few days later he was down to roughly seven thousand men. The loyalists and Indians marching with him were increasingly disinclined to continue on; many departed, leaving him mostly with British regulars and German mercenaries. In his path was a growing American army under Gates, who had recently replaced Schuyler. Initially Gates only had a few thousand under his command. His numbers swelled to over eleven thousand, primarily militia, along with a few experienced regiments of Continentals—some sent by Washington at the risk of weakening his own army. Gates chose his ground at Saratoga. Burgoyne tried to dislodge him and failed twice, first at the Battle of Freeman's Farm on September 19, then again in basically the same place before being driven back to his own defensive positions at the Battle of Bemis Heights on October 7. Belatedly he attempted to retreat. He did not get far and surrendered to Gates ten days later. It became the first significant field victory for the Americans since the fighting had begun back in April 1775.

Many of the five thousand British regulars and German mercenaries who surrendered with Burgoyne never saw home again. Burgoyne himself did; he defended himself in the House of Commons as he complained about Howe abandoning him. His troops initially were marched to Massachusetts with the expectation of returning to Britain. After Congress decided that the terms of Gates's surrender would not be honored by London, these men of the so-called "convention army" were then marched as prisoners all the way to Virginia. Eventually they were moved to Maryland, then into Pennsylvania. By war's end most had escaped into the countryside, some even settling among their former enemies. Others had been exchanged or paroled. Though not all fared as well, overall they did not suffer the indignities visited upon American prisoners of war unfortunate enough to be held in the hulks anchored off Long Island.

A relief force had sailed up the Hudson toward Burgoyne but never reached him. And it was not composed of the twelve thousand plus troops discussed over the winter. Rather, there were perhaps three thousand because Howe took so many of the twenty thousand still in New York when he decided to concentrate on beating Washington and seizing Philadelphia. General Henry Clinton, who commanded the much reduced Hudson River column, captured a couple of forts and fought through the patriots in his path, but turned back well before he even reached Albany. He knew that Burgoyne was in trouble; he also feared leaving an under-defended New York City in his rear, and not being in a position to assist Howe. By the time he turned around, Burgoyne had already surrendered anyway.

Meanwhile, Howe may have begun his campaign as a comedy of errors but it ended with him outmaneuvering his foe and capturing the American capital. He went back and forth on how to approach Philadelphia: by land or by water? Either way, the object was to draw out Washington from his Morristown hideaway, defeat him soundly, then take Philadelphia. For all of his preparations, beginning in February, Howe was not finally in position to engage the Americans until August. By then he was in southern Pennsylvania. In between he had marched his troops into New Jersey, marched them back out and put them on ships to sail up the Delaware, put them back on land, then back on the ships. After reaching the mouth of the Delaware he reconsidered his approach again, sailed south into the Chesapeake then north to where Washington, bemused by all of Howe's movements and counter-movements, prepared to intercept him.

The Americans may have been better at soldiering than they were the year before but they were still not good enough. Howe's fifteen thousand embarrassed Washington's eleven thousand at the Battle of Brandywine Creek on September 11. Washington retreated and Howe occupied Philadelphia two weeks later. A week before that, part of Howe's army humiliated part of

Washington's at Paoli. Washington struck back at Germantown on October 4, a probing attack to see how difficult it would be to dislodge Howe. The battle started fairly well for the Americans but ended with a disordered retreat. Washington trudged west to Valley Forge. Howe thought about trying to finish the job in early December, reconsidered, and prepared to winter in Philadelphia, the Royal Navy having cleared the Delaware of resistance in November.

Thus 1777 saw one great American victory and one humiliating American defeat; likewise for the British. This can hardly be characterized as a quid pro quo, however, because it was in no sense an even exchange. The Americans gained more by their victory than the British did in theirs. Strategically, occupying Philadelphia had little impact on the war. Howe held the city; he did not control the countryside. Few revolutionaries were disheartened by the loss of their new national capital, since they had no particular attachment to it and were just beginning to think in terms of a nation as something more than a coalition against the common foe.

Most crucially, Washington had been beaten again but his army had not been destroyed. And though he had no Trenton to point to at the end of the year, the same dynamic applied as in 1776: his survival meant that Britain was not winning convincingly. The rebellion that had become the Revolution continued and the disastrous outcome at Saratoga underscored that Britain could actually lose. Even Lord North began to wonder if Britain would prevail. His critics became more vocal than ever. The longer that a decisive victory eluded them, the more weary Britons would become and the more likely that the Americans would find European allies willing to take advantage of Britain's difficulties. The first signs of the defeatism— among Britons rather than Americans—that would become pronounced after Yorktown four years later were beginning to appear even now.

That France entered the war in 1778 allied to the Americans was only the most obvious reason for the growing disillusionment. The French had been contemplating entering the fray long before Saratoga. And besides, it was what the alliance represented that mattered more—proof that Britain was diplomatically isolated, with rivals only too willing to take advantage of its difficulties, even before the shooting had started. In effect, France had always been in the war. So had other European powers.

Chapter 5

Transatlantic Gambits

Arming a Nation

Anticipating war is not the same as being ready to fight it. In the months after Congress named Washington commander-in-chief and formed the rudiments of an army, it created medical and quartermaster departments as well. It also called for a Continental Navy and, not long after that, for a Marine Corps as a component part of that navy. American leaders more or less used Britain as the organizational model for their naval as well as their land forces to battle against Britain. But actually acquiring or building ships for the navy, like fielding an army, was enormously challenging. Congress would never be able to fund even half of the vessels that it wanted to have built. By war's end almost all of those that were launched had been sunk, captured or driven from the seas. That the navy existed at all, and, like the Continental Army, was formed before the nation, is nonetheless important. While the army struggled to do anything in Canada in the spring of 1776, the Continental Navy had engaged in successful commerce raiding, provided escorts for small merchant convoys, and had taken the war to the enemy that March, with a daring munitions raid on Nassau in the Bahamas. That there was almost no successful amphibious operation to match it thereafter is more of a commentary on inadequate resources than an unwillingness to engage the enemy.

Even recruiting competent physicians and obtaining medical supplies was no easy matter. Indeed, Revolutionary Americans would never have quite enough of anything they needed to wage war. Here is an instance where a disadvantage worked in their favor: their inability to keep large armies in the field helped contain the problems that they had with malnutrition and contagious diseases like smallpox and dysentery. Most often the shortages of food and clothing suffered by American soldiers, especially in the winter, were logistical. The supplies existed but Congress did not have the money to purchase them or the wherewithal to get them to the troops. Munitions shortages tended to be more literal—which is not to say that those charged with supplying the troops could always afford what little was available.

With no sure source of income, Congress had to rely on a requisition system for supplies. It set quotas; the provinces—after they supported independence, states—had the responsibility of filling them. At least there was some experience with operating in this fashion during the French and Indian War. But the supply and logistical problems that complicated the war effort then were compounded during the War of Independence. Paper money that Congress printed depreciated in such a downward spiral that we have been left with the phrase "not worth a continental dollar" to indicate just how far it fell. There were too many instances where Americans "impressed"—that is, confiscated without compensation—supplies that the British would have paid for, which worked against building support for the patriot cause.

The rapid response of Massachusetts militiamen in April 1775 should not leave the impression that the colonists were ready for war—that most future Continentals or militiamen owned weapons in good repair, knew how to use them, and had powder and shot in hand. Muskets were in such short supply that for the first couple of years they were "hired" by the Continental Army; meaning, soldiers brought their own guns and left them behind when their term of enlistment ended. There were hundreds of gunsmiths around the colonies and yet there may not have been a single powder mill operating in 1775. Therefore the stakes in those political battles over who, the king or the people, owned the munitions in public storehouses around the colonies were higher than we sometimes appreciate. Guns and ammunition for troops ideally meant standardized production—according to pre-industrial notions of precision, that is—which is not how most colonial gunsmiths plied their trade. It is not that the British made their guns and ammunition in large factories. They too used small shops working under contract. But they were used to coordinating their efforts, with a logistical system already adapted to the needs of a professional army and navy. The Americans had to learn through trial and error.

Congress created a Board of War and Ordnance in June 1776, on the eve of independence and the establishment of a nominally national army. Although the board made a game attempt at specifying what ought to be produced, it had no quality control over what was actually made. Congress put within the board's purview two magazines for storing and repairing weapons, with one established at Carlisle, Pennsylvania, and the other at Springfield, Massachusetts. Congress also provided for a commissary of military stores to coordinate obtaining and stockpiling supplies for the Continental Army.

Congress never took full control of munitions manufacture or purchasing. It left specifications, cost, production, and distribution to the states. The states delegated most of that responsibility to towns and counties. There were some attempts to erect publicly owned powder mills and even have gunsmiths on government salaries working in their own shops. In some instances skilled workmen received exemptions from military service to keep production going. Most often Congress and the states opted for a private contract system. With the loose coordination that resulted, continental and militia units could find themselves in competition for scarce supplies, which drove up prices most could already ill-afford to pay. Any attempt to establish production quotas and set price limits caused gunsmiths and powder makers to complain that the new state governments were every bit as restrictive, even as oppressive, as their old British masters. Add to that accusations of profiteering, since both Congress and the states paid commissions to those who could arrange munitions contracts.

Congress was not as desperate for new weapons by 1778 as it had been earlier, but that year it did enter into negotiations with a private French firm to set up shop somewhere along the Atlantic coast. The French would bring over skilled craftsmen to manufacture cannons, small arms, and gunpowder. They would also employ Americans who could learn the trade and branch off on their own after the war. In return the French wanted a monopoly on U.S. government arms purchases, land with trees that could be cut into gun stocks and artillery carriages, and iron ore deposits for musket and cannon barrels. Their factories would also need to be situated on a river to power water-driven machinery. Congress drew up the contract, which then fell through. The French government would not allow skilled workmen to emigrate. Besides, the French were already providing their new American allies with munitions. They had been in collusion with private parties who had been aiding and abetting the Americans since very early in the war.

It has been estimated that over a third of the gunpowder used by American soldiers came from foreign sources, primarily France. During the first two years of fighting, before American powder mills were up and running, that total was considerably higher, though attempting to give the totals now involves a great deal of guesswork about conditions then. Well over fifty thousand muskets came from foreign sources as well. If the estimates that one hundred and fifty thousand to two hundred thousand men served as continentals or militiamen are correct, that could mean that at least a quarter of them carried muskets imported during the war. Americans began making their own cannons before the war ended but initially they were completely dependent on what they could import from European suppliers or capture on American battlefields. That so many blue uniforms were imported from France no doubt helps to explain why blue had become the standard coat color in continental regiments by 1779.

Illicit Aid

When Congress called for the Continental Association back in October 1774, it fully expected provincial conventions, counties, and towns to make exceptions for the importation of war matériel. And they did. That same month the king-in-council ordered that no munitions be exported from

Britain to the colonies. With king and Congress preparing for war even as they sought to avoid it, it may have become inevitable.

The colonists had a distinct advantage in any battle over control of the Atlantic trade. After all, they had been smuggling for generations. The British, even with the largest navy in the world, could not patrol every American inlet and bay or blockade every port in Europe and the West Indies to cut off the flow of munitions to the rebels. Guns and ammunition that trickled in before the fighting began became a continuous flow thereafter. French, Dutch, and Spanish merchants all joined in the illicit wartime trade. So did some Swedes and even merchants in the Danish West Indies. Commercial connections made between American trading houses and merchants, including Britons, in the entire north Atlantic basin could easily be adapted to handling new cargoes. Some transactions were strictly cash and carry; others relied on credit established in more peaceful times.

In September 1775 Congress established a committee to coordinate the purchase of arms abroad, with Benjamin Franklin becoming its most active member. The following spring Congress dispatched Silas Deane to France to negotiate contracts there. Franklin followed before the year was out, joining Deane and Arthur Lee, who crossed over to Paris from London. Congress sent out various other agents as well, the most successful of whom was William Bingham, a Philadelphia merchant who took up residence in Martinique. Congress had authorized the committee to import one million pounds of gunpowder, ten thousand muskets, twenty thousand gunlocks (for additional muskets) and forty field pieces. With so little money in congressional coffers, the committee worked out shipments where goods could be exchanged in kind: American lumber, grain, tobacco, and fish in exchange for munitions, either directly from Europe or routed through West Indian ports. The competition could be stiff, with American agents representing individual merchants or governmental agencies competing with each other for precious cargoes. Naturally their competition inflated prices.

Some of what came out of Europe and the West Indies was pure private enterprise on the part of the sellers. But much of it involved government complicity, most often in turning a blind eye to contraband trade that violated all of the rules of international law for the legitimate behavior of neutral nations in time of war. In some of that illicit trade foreign governments were actually directly involved. Dutch-owned St. Eustatius in the West Indies was known by the British to be a clearing house for the contraband weapons trade before the end of 1774. Dutch authorities disingenuously claimed to be unaware of any illegal transactions occurring there. Others did not bother to feign ignorance. American merchant Oliver Pollock, who lived in New Orleans, purchased munitions from European and West Indian sources, then had them transported overland into South Carolina. He did so with the full knowledge of Don Bernardo de Galvez, governor of Spanish Louisiana.

The most ambitious effort to combine private enterprise with secret government aid came in the form of Roderique Hortalez et Cie., a dummy mercantile firm created in the summer of 1776. Two men were the moving force behind it: Pierre-Augustin Caron de Beaumarchais, a French playwright best remembered for *The Barber of Seville* and *The Marriage of Figaro*; and the Comte de Vergennes, the diplomat who in 1763 had predicted the American crisis. He now held the post of France's foreign minister, to which Louis XVI had appointed him not long after his accession to the throne. Beaumarchais was a true enthusiast for the American cause. Vergennes would help only insofar as American success aided France in its balance of power competition with Britain. Much of what Beaumarchais did before contacting the royal court in Versailles is shrouded in mystery. He appears to have been seeking ways to slip European munitions to American rebels almost as soon as he heard about the first clashes in Massachusetts. Benjamin Franklin had already left for home by then but Beaumarchais met with other Americans in London as he cast about for support.

The Hortalez company eventually received cash from the French government, matching funds from Spain, and some backing from French merchants. Knowing that the Americans needed munitions more than money at that point in the conflict, Vergennes smoothed the way for Beaumarchais to purchase surplus munitions from various French arsenals. By the end of 1776 Beaumarchais and his agents had assembled a truly impressive array: 300,000 pounds of gunpowder, over 200 cannons and 50,000 round shot for them, 30,000 muskets, uniforms for 25,000 men, and a long list of incidentals. Nothing else from abroad supplied to the American cause would ever come close to matching it, including what the patriots were able to arrange with the French once they were formally allied.

Privately owned merchantmen carrying those stocks did not finally cross the Atlantic until the following spring. Some docked in the French West Indies, where their large cargoes were broken up and taken to the American mainland in smaller coasting vessels. Three ships carrying the lion's share of munitions threaded their way through British patrols and arrived safely at Portsmouth, New Hampshire. Ultimately, most of the muskets and gunpowder found their way into the hands of men serving under Horatio Gates. Without those supplies the subsequent victory at Saratoga may not have been possible. That fact alone should underscore the international nature of the conflict from the beginning and serve as a reminder of an irony overlooked by simple generalizations; namely, that the American victory at Saratoga may have helped set the date for official French entry into the war, but if the French had not already been involved unofficially, then that turning point may not have been reached. It is an embarrassing footnote to the Beaumarchais story that the Americans and French disagreed over the nature of the agreement and the various shipments made through Beaumarchais's arrangements. Americans saw the supplies as a type of gift requiring no compensation; the French saw them as a loan that ought to be repaid. The U.S. government would haggle over it with Beaumarchais's heirs for two generations before paying compensation.

Marriage of Convenience

Before sailing for Philadelphia in the spring of 1775 Franklin had written an anonymous piece for the London press, warning Britain that crisis loomed, a crisis of its own making. Because its policies had alienated the colonists, war could erupt between them. Britain should not expect help from any European power to put down an American rebellion. On the contrary, it should not be surprised if those nations—all of whom had suffered at the hands of Britain as it grew in might—helped the Americans resist. Franklin's warning echoed warnings that had been offered in protest literature about Britain's American policies on both sides of the Atlantic, warnings also expressed on the floor in parliament since the days of the Stamp Act crisis. Even concerned colonists who had never been abroad understood the international implications of a rift in the British empire. Indeed, expectations that they could turn the balance of competition between Britain and its rivals to their favor probably emboldened some colonists when they began their protests.

Britain's success in the French and Indian War only complicated its diplomatic relations. It had few allies in the European community. Portugal stood out as one, but only because the Portuguese wanted to be able to turn to Britain if pressured by an overbearing Spain. Relations had cooled between Britain and Prussia, its onetime ally on the continent. The changing relations between Prussia, Austria, and Russia, part of a changing dynamic on the continent, almost marginalized Britain in matters there. Britain sought an alliance with Russia; it could only secure some commercial concessions. Russia was far more concerned with Poland and the Ottoman empire than Atlantic affairs, so it gave a higher priority to negotiations with Prussia as a counter-balance to Austria and even France. France looked with alarm when a Russian fleet sailed from the Baltic into the Mediterranean to demonstrate its growing ambitions and to announce that eastern Europe was no longer a political backwater.

Competition with France and concern over whether Spain would march to France's tune continued to be Britain's greatest concern. France annexed Corsica in 1768, which Britain decided not to oppose or interpret as a threat to the balance of power in the Mediterranean. There would be various flare-ups with France after the 1763 treaty, from India to the coast of Africa and into the Caribbean. None reached the level of danger of Britain's dispute with Spain over the Falkland Islands in 1770–1771, which took both countries to the brink of war. Britain's interest in this South Atlantic island group was as a stepping-stone to the west. As the exploring expeditions of James Cook bracketing these years demonstrated, Britain's desire to tie together the Atlantic and Pacific in a grand worldwide trade network was growing. Spain, fearing that what it viewed as its Pacific lake was about to be invaded, was startled into activity. Even so, France made it clear that it had no interest in going to war alongside Spain over this particular set of disputed claims. Spain, no match for Britain at sea, negotiated rather than go to war.

Despite having renewed their Family Compact, the Bourbon powers did not often work in concert and neither looked for an excuse to challenge Britain directly. Britain's relative diplomatic isolation only became problematical as the American crisis deepened and old enemies eventually found a unique opportunity to take revenge and perhaps level the international playing field.

Rebellious colonists knew that seeking foreign aid was one thing; obtaining a foreign alliance without declaring independence was quite another. Thomas Paine had argued in *Common Sense* that Americans in an independent republic could be freed from the wars that marked monarchies, substituting bloodless competition in the marketplace for the blood of a battlefield. "It is the true interest of America to steer clear of European contentions," Paine proclaimed. Once out from under Britain's thumb, the United States could chart a new diplomatic course. In Paine's brave new world, nations who, because of Britain, had thought of Americans as enemies would now consider them friends. In a war that was already replete with irony, another could be added: Paine wanted Revolutionary Americans to take advantage of traditional international balance of power politics to alter that very system, the old age making possible the new.

Benjamin Franklin knew it would not be that simple. True, the wording of the proposed treaty with France that Congress approved in September 1776 called for "universal Peace" and "true and sincere Friendship" between the two nations. But that was diplomatic boilerplate, not some new approach to international relations being proposed by the new nation. The rest was very pragmatic and very specific, guaranteeing each party most favored nation trade privileges and promises to protect each other's commerce from seizure by any third party. Congress included the phrase that "free ships make free goods," a notion long-championed by the Dutch. To balance that assertion it also included a long list of contraband articles that could not be carried to an enemy. The United States was to have a free hand in North America; France the same in the West Indies. If Britain declared war on France as a result of this treaty, the United States promised not to side with Britain. In brief, Congress laid out commercial connections in detail and deliberately left the possibility of a more binding political and military alliance vague.

Even though Congress had decided that "it is expedient forthwith to make the most effectual measures for foreign alliances," John Adams and many of his colleagues had misgivings. Commercial connections seemed less binding and ultimately less complicated than political ties. When contemplating the latter, choosing the "expedient" determined both French and American behavior. In appealing to the people of Canada to join in common cause, as when approaching the French government to obtain financial and material aid, all anti-French rhetoric had to be put aside. That was easier for some than for others. One prominent Boston minister dusted off a sermon that he had given during the previous war and made the necessary edits while keeping the basic text the same: the bad French were now good, the good British, bad. A cynic would dismiss such role switching as mere political opportunism; a realist accepts that life can take strange turns.

The French kept the Americans at arm's length until near the end of 1777. Even if war was not, as historian H. M. Scott put it, "inevitable" by the summer of 1777, Versailles and London were preparing for it. By then France's naval rebuilding program, a priority since the British had decimated a French fleet at Quiberon Bay in 1759, had achieved its purposes. A few months later at Saratoga the Americans proved they could win. At the Brandywine and Germantown they showed that they would not fall apart with defeat.

Vergennes knew it was most unlikely that Americans would renounce independence, reconcile with Britain, and then, together, turn on France. His patience rewarded, Vergennes persuaded a hesitant Louis XVI that the time was finally right for direct intervention. Two treaties were signed in February 1778. The military alliance created in one has received the most attention. The commercial relations set up in the other, which strengthened trade ties and opened the door for more direct financial assistance, was equally important. One basically repeated most of the terms the Americans had written into their model treaty, with some provisions carried into the other. That other treaty bound the two nations in an alliance in the event of Britain declaring war on France, committing them to assist each other in achieving victory and not negotiating a separate peace. A clause aimed primarily at Spain was inserted inviting other nations wronged by Britain to join the pact. The French had already assembled an expeditionary force for the colonies before Congress ratified the treaties in May. France actually declared war against Britain first, in July, after naval clashes in the channel and just as its fleet arrived in American waters.

The Long Road to Yorktown

It would take the French and Americans three years to bring their combined force to bear—because theirs was always an uneasy partnership and because achieving a decisive victory proved elusive. The British knew about the French plans well in advance, evacuated Philadelphia and prepared New York for attack. The French admiral, d'Estaing, thought better of trying to dislodge them. With the broadening of the war General Henry Clinton, Howe's replacement, had to shift resources about. He sent some of his troops, with naval support, to the West Indies, where the French could be expected to strike at some point. In June 1778 Clinton had marched the bulk of his troops across New Jersey in an orderly retreat, though Washington had emerged from winter quarters at Valley Forge with renewed energy. Compared with earlier open field engagements, his troops did well in the subsequent clash at Monmouth Courthouse. They were not able to prevent Clinton from reaching the safety of New York, but, with the training they had received from Baron von Steuben over the winter months, they showed that they could stand their ground if well led and effectively equipped.

Washington's army, unable to get at the British on Manhattan, Staten Island or western Long Island, formed a loose ring around the British. Even with growing French assistance Washington would never have sufficient strength to retake the city proper. While the patriots spent years in an impotent siege, the war in the West had erupted with greater violence—on the New York frontier, over the Appalachians in the future Kentucky and Tennessee, and even much closer to long-settled white communities in the Wyoming Valley of Pennsylvania. As fighting intensified, both the British and the Americans had hoped to secure native allies in all of those areas. The British had more success and were able to combine Indians and loyalist militia, from both Canada and New York, into large-scale raiding parties. Revolutionary Americans, generally unable to attract Indian allies beyond some Delaware and Oneida warriors, then hoped that most other Indians would remain neutral. They enjoyed little success there either. They did launch an ambitious 1779 campaign to intimidate the Iroquois in New York and various tribes in western Pennsylvania into submission. General John Sullivan commanded one expedition into Indian country, Colonel Daniel Brodhead another. They destroyed villages and crops and dispersed the natives for a time. They also deepened animosities that would cripple Indian–white relations into the postwar years.

George Rogers Clark's more famous 1778–1779 incursion into the Illinois country enjoyed some success but could not break the native connection with the British in Detroit, much less take the offensive to Detroit itself. The war that Clark carried north across the Ohio River spread back into Kentucky, the "dark and bloody ground" whose control was still being contested at the war's end. That the British included lands west of the Appalachians and east of the Mississippi in the area ceded to the new United States in 1783 because of Clark's campaign is largely a myth.

If, on the frontier, Revolutionary Americans barely held their own, on the coast they fared even worse. The British finally began their long-delayed campaign to restore imperial authority to the South. Starting with a fairly small expeditionary force they took Savannah before the end of 1778. They then shifted additional men and resources to an even more ambitious campaign in the Carolinas. They captured Charleston in May 1780 and the following August defeated a relief force sent by Washington under Horatio Gates at Camden.

Camden, we now know, would mark the low point of Revolutionary American military fortunes. All of South Carolina and Georgia lay exposed, ripe for pacification and restoration of imperial authority. Not only had Savannah fallen in December 1778 but also a combined Franco-American operation to retake it the next fall did not succeed, the allies showing that they did not work well together—as in the previous year, when they proved unable to collaborate against the British in Rhode Island. The British had since then decided to withdraw from Newport. In their eyes it was no more significant than having pulled out of Boston and Philadelphia in earlier years. Strategic withdrawal did not mean impending defeat; rather, it signified a shift in emphasis south—toward the Carolinas and Virginia, and toward the West Indies, where rival fleets jockeyed for position. Washington lay encamped outside New York, unable to take the city. There would be fighting along the Hudson and on Staten Island by sizeable units, but nothing changed the local balance of power. Only in New England could the revolution be considered secure. Whitehall and Westminster finally gave up any thought of reclaiming the region.

What looked so bleak in the fall of 1780 turned much brighter almost exactly a year later. The American cause was helped immensely by the failure of Henry Clinton and Charles Cornwallis to coordinate their efforts. They came close to replaying the mistakes of Howe and Burgoyne nearly four years before. In 1777 Howe, at least, had Philadelphia and a stymied Washington to show for his efforts, even if he left Burgoyne to his own devices. In 1781 Clinton, by contrast, would have nothing to show for himself and Cornwallis would have Yorktown as his unwanted claim on our memory. Blamed by some for the confused 1777 campaign, Germain largely left Clinton and Cornwallis alone.

Clinton had commanded in the 1780 campaign that led to the fall of Charleston. He then returned to New York, leaving Cornwallis to carry forward the pacification program that was succeeding in Georgia into the Carolinas. Cornwallis did indeed begin the process, with Charleston, like Savannah, once again trading within the empire and with a local government that had sworn allegiance to crown and empire. The loyalty oaths initiated by the patriots to drive loyalists out or underground were turned around and did the same to them. But rather than consolidate his coastal control, Cornwallis chose to press inland and then north, to sweep the Carolinas free of rebel influence and to clear the way for a push into Virginia. There he would join with smaller forces already operating in the Chesapeake. If Washington left the New York highlands with his main army to contest control, he and Clinton would crush him—as had been the plan for 1777. But as in 1777 with Howe and Burgoyne, Cornwallis and Clinton communicated badly, each leading the other to misunderstand circumstances on the ground and the range of possible choices—until, again, it was too late.

After driving off the Americans at Camden, Cornwallis thought he would encounter little organized resistance as he went north. He advanced in two columns, with a thousand or so men under Major Patrick Ferguson on his left while he commanded the main force, perhaps twice as large. He had a core of British regulars under him, with a smattering of loyalists. Ferguson had virtually all loyalists, most from the Carolinas, with a mix from New York and New Jersey. He sought to intimidate the locals. Instead, Carolinians, with help drawn from as far away as Virginia and "over the mountain" men from Tennessee, converged and rushed forward, a thousand strong, crushing him at King's Mountain on October 7, 1780. Ferguson was slain and his force swallowed whole. Just under a dozen of Ferguson's men were hanged as war criminals after a drumhead court martial. Their fate is a reminder that some of the most unforgiving fighting of the entire war was between white Americans. They could be as brutal toward each other as the more familiar tales of frontier warfare or the actions of European mercenaries against American militia.

Cornwallis fell back, paused, then, with some reinforcements sent by Clinton from New York, decided to press forward in January 1781. He would now be up against General Nathanael Greene, who was far more imaginative and resourceful than Gates had been. Once again Cornwallis advanced in two columns, the left flank this time under the command of Banastre Tarleton. About a thousand strong, Tarleton's force was composed of infantry and cavalry, primarily British but with some Americans. Denounced as "Bloody Tarleton" for the actions of his troops at the Waxhaws, Tarleton has come to symbolize the brutal nature of the warfare in the Southern theatre, especially after Gates's defeat eliminated the presence of American regulars in South Carolina. Both sides engaged in stubborn, vendetta-driven, guerrilla warfare, matching, even exceeding, that already seen in New York and New Jersey. Partisans—most famously Francis Marion, Andrew Pickens, and Thomas Sumter for the revolutionaries—in forces ranging from a few dozen to several hundred, raided and burned their way through the countryside. In sum, war as Tarleton waged it was all too typical.

On January 17 at the Cowpens, Tarleton's men suffered a fate similar to Ferguson's. In a battlefield plan often celebrated as the most ingenious of the war, General Daniel Morgan had arranged his mix of continentals and militia to maximize their strengths and minimize their weaknesses. He positioned his militia armed with rifles out front and militia carrying muskets behind them. They had orders to fall back on his most reliable continentals as the enemy advanced. He had a small cavalry force in reserve. A combination of skill and luck netted him over eight hundred of Tarleton's men as killed, wounded, or prisoners, although Tarleton himself escaped on horseback.

Cornwallis pursued Greene and Morgan into North Carolina, trying (and failing) to catch them before they could combine forces, then trying (and failing) to crush them. Greene took his army all the way into Virginia, then turned back into North Carolina to meet Cornwallis. At over four thousand men—most of them militia—Greene outnumbered Cornwallis nearly two-to-one. Cornwallis won a costly victory at Guilford Courthouse on March 15. He held the field but soon left, having suffered more casualties than Greene. Too weak to continue north or return overland south, he retreated east to Wilmington. Whatever loyalist support he had had melted away. Greene lost most of the local militia who had turned out in his support too, but some returned to him when he reversed course back south. In a campaign that stretched all the way into September, with various engagements culminating in the Battle of Eutaw Springs, Greene, assisted by still active partisans, undid pacification in the Carolina countryside. He suffered a string of tactical defeats even as he achieved strategic victory. The British fell back on Charleston and Savannah, which they would not evacuate for many months to come. But by then it had long been clear that the revolutionaries had regained the initiative and the king's southernmost provinces, never fully restored to him, were possibly lost for good.

Cornwallis had slogged on to meet what we now too often think of as his date with destiny at Yorktown. But Cornwallis, like his adversaries, was not fated to do anything. Though he would suffer the consequences of poor choices and bad breaks, the outcome was in no sense pre-determined. Clinton had previously sent two small expeditionary forces into the Chesapeake, not to pave the way for Cornwallis, but to secure a naval base of operations to better support the campaign in the Carolinas and provide yet another link to the West Indies. He did not share Cornwallis's ambitions to take Virginia, especially at the cost of pacification to the south. He was actually more interested in taking the fighting back up the Delaware to Philadelphia; he certainly had no intention of abandoning New York, whatever Cornwallis had in mind.

Combining all of the forces at his disposal, Cornwallis had roughly eight thousand men—mostly British regulars, with some German mercenaries and loyalist provincial units. He could not count on any local loyalists to join him. His opponents, by contrast, could expect local militia support. Von Steuben, the Marquis de Lafayette, and General Anthony Wayne had all brought continentals with them to Virginia. Just as in 1777, Washington willingly parted with valued troops if he thought they could be better deployed elsewhere. The continentals linked up with militiamen, some of whom had fought at King's Mountain. Cornwallis had struck as far west as Charlottesville before they could converge, but then Cornwallis went east, isolating himself on a peninsula, with Yorktown as his base. He assumed that Clinton would either join forces with him or evacuate his command

and shift operations elsewhere. He was in place by August; he would not leave until October, having surrendered his entire army.

In what is rightly admired as the most successful combined operation of the war, Washington and his French allies trapped Cornwallis before he could escape or be reinforced by Clinton. In part they succeeded because Cornwallis and Clinton did not communicate effectively, nor did the British generals coordinate with the British admirals commanding fleets close by in New York or at a greater distance in the West Indies. But in large part they lost because of superior Franco-American planning and execution. The allies had essentially two months to carry off their plans, which meant shifting troops in New York over four hundred miles south, to link up with two French fleets, one dropping down from Rhode Island, the other sailing up from the West Indies. Neither Clinton nor Cornwallis realized until too late what Washington was about. Washington worked closely with General Rochambeau, whose five thousand French troops had joined him in New York, then marched with him for Virginia. Admiral de Barras, commanding a French squadron stationed at Newport, sailed south to the Chesapeake. There he linked up with Admiral de Grasse, whose even larger fleet, with several thousand troops on board, arrived from the West Indies.

The French drove off a combined British fleet, effectively sealing the Chesapeake. Battered behind his breastworks at Yorktown, Cornwallis attempted, then abandoned, a last minute escape across the York River to Gloucester—to go where, it was not clear. His situation hopeless, he surrendered on October 19. Washington's seventeen thousand man army had been half French, half American, and only half of those Americans were continentals. The navy was entirely French; the siege guns that pounded the British into submission were largely French; many of the weapons carried by the Americans, even the uniforms they wore, had been made in France; most of the money that funded the campaign came from France as well. Americans tend to think of the campaign as Washington's victory, gained with French assistance. The reality is more stark: if there had been no French aid, no larger international conflict, there would have been no Yorktown at all.

Yorktown ended a campaign; it did not end the war. Thrilled as Washington was with the victory, he wished that de Grasse would have stayed longer—that they could dash south and seize Wilmington or perhaps be more ambitious and strike at Charleston. Far too much has been made of North's outburst, upon hearing of Cornwallis's surrrender, "Oh God! It is all over." The king did not feel that way, nor did Germain, nor, for several more months, did most members of parliament. North had been worrying that the war was unwinnable since the end of 1777 and offered to resign even then. Ending the war with Yorktown—which all too many American histories do—can reflect a view that concentrates too much on

North America and not enough on the larger world conflict, too much on land campaigns and not enough on what happened at sea.

As the noted British historian Piers Mackesy contended, the British still had military options that they chose not to exercise. Winding down the war after Yorktown was a political choice, not a military necessity. The British had thirty thousand troops in North America. They held St. Augustine, Savannah, Charleston, and New York in the areas caught up in rebellion. Canada was securely in their hands, the rebels having been ejected in 1776. American plans for a second invasion after France entered the war had been abandoned. The rebels never threatened Nova Scotia and, to the west in the Maine country, had been humiliated at Penobscot Bay. The British had clear naval supremacy in that entire theater of operations, with the ability to choose a coastal striking point.

Some war enthusiasts in Britain and diehard loyalists on site urged new campaigns, pointing out, rightly, that if Clinton and Cornwallis had not squandered their gains, the southern campaign could have succeeded. Pacification might still work; imperial authority might still be restored to the Carolina tidewater and strengthened in Georgia. With perhaps a bit more fighting Britain could negotiate a peace that would confine an independent United States to an area east of the Appalachians, south of Canada, west of Penobscot Bay in Maine and no lower than the Chesapeake. With boundaries so narrow and prospects so bleak, how long would it be before independent Americans begged to be brought back into the empire?

Reconsiderations

True enough, Cornwallis's surrender at Yorktown was not Britain's only setback in 1781. The French took Tobago; Minorca was under siege by a joint French and Spanish force; the Spanish, operating out of Havana, took Pensacola, following their success at Mobile the year before. Those setbacks followed others in the West Indies that had already underscored Britain's precarious position: it no longer enjoyed the naval superiority that it once took for granted. The British had already had to abandon plans to begin building their strength in the Pacific, as the French challenged them in India and the Dutch posed a threat in East Asia. The Spanish had entered the war in 1779, allied to the French but not the Americans. They did not leap at the opportunity provided by war to settle old scores; they chose their moment carefully. They had made restoration of Gibraltar, which the British captured in 1704, the price of their neutrality. Only after being rebuffed by the British did they join the hostilities, with the hope of retaking Gibraltar and possibly the Floridas. Although the French assisted the Spanish in eventually taking Minorca, their combined operation to invade England in 1779 never came off. French and Spanish warships maneuvered about the Channel opposite Britain's home fleet, but the troops gathered in northern France never set sail for their targets on the Isle of Wight and Portsmouth.

At the end of 1780 the Netherlands too entered the contest, not allied to the French or Spanish, much less the Americans. Earlier that year the Dutch had signed onto the League of Armed Neutrality formed by Catherine the Great of Russia. Denmark and Sweden had joined with Russia as well, along with Prussia and Austria. Even Portugal would join but only after the Americans and British had begun peace negotiations. France and Spain were nominally involved in what has been derided as the "armed nullity." The Americans were not invited to join Catherine's league, despite their efforts to be included. No European power after France in 1778 would recognize American independence until the Dutch agreed to a commercial treaty in October 1782, after peace negotiations between the British and the Americans had already begun.

The League was not formed as a military alliance seeking war with Britain; rather, member nations agreed to defend the rights of neutral carriers during war. Determining those rights could be extremely complicated, particularly when ships, cargoes, and destinations could be intermixed—such as Swedish goods carried on a Dutch vessel to a Russian port. Members of the League wanted those rights to be broadly construed. Britain, the League's obvious diplomatic target, wanted those rights to be more narrowly confined, which entailed a looser definition of what could be considered contraband. League members, with their naval patrols in the Baltic and North Sea, did not pose that much of a threat to Britain's war effort. American privateers, some of which operated out of French ports, did, accounting for hundreds of captured prizes. The exploits of John Paul Jones for the Continental Navy did not pose the same sort of challenge but did have some shock value and were part of the cumulative effects producing British war weariness.

In the closing days of 1780, Catherine the Great had thought that she might be called upon to mediate an end to the fighting. There were both Britons and Americans sympathetic to the idea of mediation, by Russia or possibly even Austria. But the British were not yet willing to recognize American independence and leading American Revolutionaries would not settle for anything less. Before Yorktown gave a boost to their confidence, 1781 had not looked like a propitious year for the Americans. It in fact opened with the mutiny of Pennsylvania's continentals, which the officers were powerless to quell. Commanded by their sergeants, the Pennsylvanians, driven to desperation by their pitiful conditions and shabby treatment by civilian authorities, had decided to take their demands to the state government and Continental Congress in Philadelphia. They were stopped, not by superior force, but by their own forbearance and their ability to distinguish between governmental failures and the higher cause. They had no interest in switching sides.

The British followed their failure at Yorktown with a nice little victory in the West Indies, reversing the trend that had emerged earlier in the fighting. The French had taken Dominica from them in 1778, St. Vincent the next year, and de Grasse's fleet, victorious in Virginia, added St. Kitts and Nevis to the spoils in January and February 1782. But French success ended when de Grasse, preparing to next attack Jamaica, ran afoul of Admiral Rodney, was beaten and taken prisoner at the Battle of the Saints in April. Whitehall, which learned of Rodney's victory in May, had already decided to cut its losses and negotiate with the Americans. The king knew that the Americans would not accept anything short of independence. The Saints gave him the excuse to pull out of negotiations but he did not take it. Only then can it be fairly said that American independence had become inevitable—though the size of the new nation and its place in the international community were by no means set.

Britain had been seeking some way to satisfy the Americans short of granting independence before they had even declared it. George III refused to deal directly with the Continental Congress until after the Franco-American alliances impressed upon him the danger of letting the rebels go too long as revolutionaries tied to a neighboring enemy. He had agreed that the Howe brothers should try to negotiate some sort of settlement even as they pressed their 1776 campaign to capture New York and defeat Washington's army. Admittedly, they were averse to prosecuting the war too vigorously, preferring that the Americans give up rather than be bloodily beaten into submission. Admiral Howe had even met with Franklin before he left London in the days before the shooting started, in unofficial discussions aimed at avoiding war. Having failed to prevent the fighting, the Howes wanted to minimize the damage and hoped that a restitution of imperial authority could be achieved, talking peace as they waged war.

The charge given to the Howe brothers would be passed down to their successors. William Howe was always a peace commissioner as well as commander of the British land forces in the colonies. So were his successors, Henry Clinton and Guy Carleton; likewise for Richard Howe and the five admirals succeeding him who commanded Britain's North American fleets through the end of the war. The Howes had been in the peculiar position of ignoring Congress, acting as if it and the state governments did not exist. The king empowered them to negotiate with any group that would form itself as an alternative to the rebel governments, swearing allegiance to crown and empire. Those spontaneously formed groups would provide the core for a restoration of legitimate government. With luck those loyalists could use revolutionary methods to reverse revolutionary results.

With hindsight we see more clearly that the odds against any such group succeeding, absent a decisive British military victory, were long indeed. One of the many counterfactual "what ifs" some historians have posed is this: would the outcome have been different if the British had chosen to use a naval blockade alone in 1775, the rebels giving up after dividing against themselves, their shared cause a shambles? So Viscount Barrington, George III's secretary at war, had advised near the end of 1774, before the shooting even started. But perhaps the greatest error in British strategic thinking was the assumption that New England was anomalous, that the rebels there had proven to be a majority who could be isolated from the more loyal colonies to the south. As Major General James Robertson testified in the House of Commons after Yorktown, he had not expected to beat rebellious Americans into submission; rather, he had expected "to assist the good Americans to subdue the bad."

Crown and parliament did authorize the Carlisle commission sent in 1778 to negotiate directly with Congress. They had become far more conciliatory, even expressing a willingness to suspend (without renouncing) the Declaratory Act and repeal much of the legislation that Americans believed had precipitated war. Though still opposed to the imperial federalism entailed in accepting an inter-colonial congress, they were receptive to the idea of individual colonies paying their share of imperial expenses through requisitions. Their hope was that Revolutionary Americans would drop their insistence on independence, that Congress would dissolve itself, and states in the nation would resume their place as provinces in the empire. But it was far too late for that. The views expressed by Franklin when dealing informally with the Howes two years before were still held by Revolutionary leaders. Britain, Franklin told the Howes two weeks after Congress declared independence, possessed too much "fondness for conquest," too great a "lust for ambition" to be trusted with protecting American rights. Revolutionary Americans wanted to be part of an empire of liberty, but one of their own making.

Whitehall and Westminster accepted that reality most reluctantly, a reluctance reflected in the resolution passed by the House of Commons on February 27, 1782. Introduced by Henry Conway, it failed on the first reading and was carried by only nineteen votes (234–215) once it did pass. It proposed ending the fighting in North America, not as a first step toward recognizing American independence, but as a means of achieving a "happy reconciliation" so that Britain could concentrate on defeating France. The resolution had no chance in the House of Lords. Nor would it be endorsed by George III. Just the opposite; the king even contemplated abdicating the throne rather than let any of his American colonies go. No one was more surprised than the king himself when disaster did not ensue because most of his American subjects had departed the empire.

Reconfigurations

The British and Americans began "secret" negotiations in April 1782. Those negotiations were not truly secret, however, and the most basic American demand—independence—was never negotiable. Benjamin Franklin and John Adams were already on the scene in Paris. They would be joined by John Jay, who had been in Madrid, and Henry Laurens, released from the Tower of London after being captured at sea. Their counterparts were Richard Oswald, then David Hartley. Both Britons admired Franklin and considered the attempt to hold the colonies in the empire by force a mistake. Neither was inclined to drive any hard bargains and, despite the fall of two ministries and formation of a third during the negotiations, directions from London remained basically unchanged.

Franklin had divided American aims into two categories: the necessary and the preferred. All of the necessary were achieved, beginning with American independence being acknowledged rather than granted. That meant the new nation could date its founding from July 1776 rather than September 1783, when the final treaty was signed, proof that it had won its freedom rather than had it bestowed. The other necessities included generous boundaries, fishing rights off of Newfoundland, and Britain's promise to withdraw all troops within American borders. Franklin's preferences had to be set aside: no Canada as part of the United States, no free trade with Britain, no British acknowledgment that it had caused the war. Canada would remain in the empire. In separate treaties, Britain lost Senegal and Tobago to France. Other West Indies islands that had changed hands were returned to their pre-war associations. France and Spain agreed to return Minorca as well, but Spain regained the Floridas, which it had lost to Britain in the 1763 treaty.

It has often been remarked that the Americans in Paris showed their mastery of realpolitik, negotiating a peace with Britain separately from France—technically a violation of the 1778 treaty, but done knowing that the French were looking for an excuse to end the war. Spain wanted to continue fighting until it had Gibraltar. American actions provided the French with an excuse to bow out and for Spain to quit. Franklin and his colleagues indeed proved adroit. Even so they were able to navigate difficult diplomatic waters because the French did not stand in their way and the British had decided to let them go.

Negotiating on their own cut both ways. Britain accepted a southern U.S. boundary along the 31st parallel and north through the middle of the Mississippi River, with the right of navigation to its mouth. Spain, which reached its own peace with Britain, was not bound by that agreement, as Americans would soon learn to their frustration. Britain gave up the Floridas to entice Spain from continuing its siege of Gibraltar. Spain had seized much of West Florida during the war. But not East Florida and the British settlers who had moved there since 1763 felt abandoned. Americans living to the north of the Floridas would, over the next generation, impinge on both; whether the territory was Spanish or British, it did not particularly matter to expansionistic Americans. And while Americans could be happy with a northern border passing through the middle of the Great Lakes, with a line drawn above Lake Champlain and including much of the Maine country, they were still suspicious of British ambitions in Canada, suspicions fed by the British not immediately evacuating military posts on what was technically American soil. Indeed, all of the fears of being hemmed in by rivals that had marked the colonial period carried over into the early National Era.

The treaty called for "perpetual peace and harmony" between the old empire and the new nation—a type of diplomatic boilerplate, but also a genuine expression of informal reconciliation. To Samuel Flagg Bemis and Charles M. Andrews, pioneers among American historians studying the American Revolution within a larger imperial context, there was something tragic about all of this. With Americans and Britons going their separate ways, they lamented, the world had lost an opportunity to see a Pax Britannica. Had they only been able to reconcile their differences, to focus on the deep-seated commonalities that joined them rather than the superficial differences that divided them, they could have built a grand transatlantic commonwealth, the foundation for a truly global empire of liberty. Avowed internationalists who wrote in the aftermath of World War I and the failure of the League of Nations to unite that postwar world, Bemis and Andrews felt that they had expressed a self-evident truth. The unspoken part of that truth is that they saw American and British tendencies as being fundamentally the same: two nations who believed in the possibility of having empires without imperialism.

Part III

Nation as Empire

Map 3 The United States in 1783. Map by Alice Thiede, CARTO-GRAPHICS

Chapter 6

Forming a More Perfect Union

Novus Ordo Seclorum

William Henry Drayton's 1776 predictions about an American empire are nearly as famous as those offered by John Adams in 1755. Adams's had been prompted by his leaving Harvard and entering the professional world, Drayton's by his presiding over a new state court in an independent nation. Joining the patriot cause in early 1775, the Oxford-educated South Carolinian became president of the provincial convention, later sat in the Continental Congress, and in between had served as the state's first chief justice. Speaking from the bench in Charleston and issuing his charge to the first grand jury to be impaneled since independence was declared, he instructed those jurors in their legal duties. But he did so in the context of the new age now upon them, as they began life in an "infant empire." Noting the fall of republican Rome and Britain's pending loss of some if not all of its American colonies, he contended that, historically, "Empires have their Zenith—and their Declension to a Dissolution." His countrymen, "no longer bound" by Britain, were now "free" to prove themselves as they took part in the "Rise of the American Empire."

"How few are the Days of true Glory," Drayton intoned; all nations share the "common Fate" of rising only to fall. But Drayton did not speak as a fatalist. He offered hope, with no hint of any apocalypse to come. As he saw it, God Himself had chosen the present generation of Americans to found a new nation and build a new empire. His countrymen had not sought independence; it had been thrust upon them as they chose freedom over slavery. How long would their new empire last? Drayton did not explicitly claim that they would escape the cycles of history and yet, after quoting the Declaration of Independence, he claimed that the American empire "bids fair, by the Blessing of God, to be the most glorious of any upon Record." Americans need only prove worthy of their providential destiny to prevail in the great struggle ahead.

An American acceptance of social forces beyond any one nation's control had always been paired uneasily with a belief that perhaps the past did not necessarily bind the future. Such dualistic thinking should be expected from a people who combined classical and Christian assumptions because both offered mixed messages about the role played by human agency. Perhaps that helps to explain the difficulty encountered when Congress chose the design for what became the Great Seal of the United States. On July 4, 1776 Congress had formed a three-man committee—John Adams, Benjamin Franklin, and Thomas Jefferson—to design it. They all had their own ideas, with Adams clearly favoring the classical, Franklin the biblical, and Jefferson combining the two. It would take several more committees and another six years before the final form could be agreed on, a form essentially unchanged in the centuries since.

The obverse, or front, of the Seal features a coat of arms emblazoned with an eagle. The eagle, wings spread, holds an olive branch symbolizing peace in its right talons and thirteen arrows symbolizing war in its left. The eagle looks toward the olive branch rather than the arrows, indicating a preference for peace. A banner inscribed "E Pluribus Unum"—out of many, one—passes through its beak. Its body is covered by a shield, with a field of blue at the top and thirteen alternating stripes, seven white, six red, under that. Over the eagle is a constellation of thirteen stars, shining forth as the United States joins the other great powers in the world. On the reverse is an unfinished pyramid, above it an all-seeing eye with the Latin phrase "Annuit Coeptus"—He has favored our undertaking—in an arc above. "Novus Ordo Seclorum"—a new order of the ages—appears below. The base of the pyramid features 1776, displayed in Roman numerals.

During the crisis leading to war, there had been those in parliament who warned against any attempt at power-sharing with the colonists. That could only result in a dreaded *imperium in imperio*—the state within a state, which confused the issue of ultimate authority even as parts were pitted against the whole. Like the Declaration of Independence, the Great Seal captured the American ambition to create a federal republic that proved wrong the old adage that sovereignty had to be indivisible. The Declaration had called the Americans "one people"; it also proclaimed that they lived in "free and independent states."

The Great Seal presented American federalism as a given, its very existence trumping the logic of earlier ages. The Seal also attempted to capture the higher purposes behind the founding, placing the new nation within the course of history—thus the Latin borrowing from Virgil—but also suggesting that the United States represented a new age, one making the rules that had governed those who came before irrelevant. Although other nations had claimed to be starting the world anew, these Americans believed they could be the first to make good on that claim. In that sense independence was the means to an end, not an end in itself. It marked the birth of a reformer nation determined to reshape itself and the larger world. "There is nothing more common than to confound" the American Revolution with the War of Independence, observed Dr. Benjamin Rush of Philadelphia. He and his countrymen had changed governments but it "remains yet to establish and perfect the principles, morals, and manners of our citizens." Rush knew that any talk of perfection, personal or collective, raised the stakes. He and other leading revolutionaries committed themselves to squaring the circle—to somehow making the impossible, possible. And yet they approached their tasks as realistic idealists. They did not seek to change human nature but, instead, to encourage what they considered desirable attributes even as they discouraged those they liked less. Whatever governmental system they devised, they wanted to draw on the best of what office holders had to offer the public without being brought down by the unscrupulous among them.

Confederation

George Washington did not necessarily share the confidence expressed in the design of the Great Seal, at least initially. A year after Congress adopted it, an exasperated Washington was still serving as commander of the American army. Although he wanted to go home to Virginia, he and his troops were once again stationed in the New York highlands while the British continued to occupy the city to the south. Congress kept him abreast of the negotiations that were leading to independence, but those peace talks were not proceeding as fast as he had hoped they would.

By June 1783 soldiers in the Pennsylvania line had mutinied again. They marched on Philadelphia and protested against their continued poor treatment. Fortunately they returned to their barracks before having to be forcibly dispersed. Just a few months before that, members of the officer corps serving with Washington at Newburgh had considered making a protest of their own. Until they received back pay and were assured that they would be given their promised pensions and grants of land, they might refuse to obey orders—whether those orders were to go home or to remain in the field. Proving to be a master of political theater, Washington shamed them by unexpectedly addressing the group. At one point, to the shock of all but those few who knew him best, he put on glasses to finish reading a letter from a member of Congress. He reportedly asked their pardon and commented, in a well-directed aside, that he had grown gray and nearly blind in their service.

Washington made it plain at Newburgh that he would have no part of any coup. The military must be subordinate to civilian authority if their experiment in republicanism were to succeed. He nonetheless felt obligated to tell state and national leaders that their new political system was in desperate need of repair. His wartime pleas for more men and more supplies were now followed with advice for the postwar world. There could be no true political independence without security, he stressed, and there could be no security without a stronger national union. The "confederated republic" would not last long without clearer lines of authority, starting with a national government capable of leading the states. If strengthened, they could cement together an American people whose nationalism, a product of the war, was about to be tested in peace. "It is in our United capacity we are known, and have a place among the Nations of the Earth," he wrote in one of his many letters from Newburgh. The "Confederated Powers" could lead the nation to greatness or let it slip into chaos. "For certain I am," he warned, "that unless adequate Powers are given to Congress for the *general* purposes of the Federal Union" the new nation "shall soon moulder into dust and become contemptible in the Eyes of Europe."

By then the nation had been governed officially under the Articles of Confederation for over two years and unofficially for four years before that. Those Articles, approved by Congress in November 1777 but not formally ratified by all of the thirteen states until March 1781, had originally been submitted to Congress less than two weeks after it declared independence. John Dickinson headed the committee that drafted it. John Adams, busy on the committee simultaneously drafting the Declaration, had been anticipating this moment for many months. "I have ever Thought it the most difficult and dangerous Part of this Business Americans have to do in this mighty Contest," he confided to Mercy Otis Warren, "to Contrive some Method in the Colonies to glide insensibly, from under the old Government, into a peaceable and contented submission to new ones."

Although Adams thought Congress ought to draft a model treaty to guide it in its dealings with foreign nations, he did not think Congress could provide a blueprint for the colonies as they drafted new state constitutions. There were too many differences that could potentially divide them and the most pressing task, at that moment, was to unify. In May 1776 Congress did call on the provinces in rebellion to reconstitute themselves governmentally, in anticipation of creating an independent nation. But given the variety of forms involved, Adams and his congressional colleagues accepted that each state should concentrate on adapting its own old institutions to new circumstances.

Congress revised Dickinson's original draft considerably before agreeing to it, reducing the twenty articles to thirteen. In a throwback to Franklin's proposal of July 1775, the confederation was characterized as a "firm league of friendship." And yet it was also obvious that something fundamental set these articles apart from Franklin's. Each colony "shall enjoy and retain as much as it may think fit of its own present Laws" Franklin had written tentatively, with each having the ability to "amend its own Constitution as shall seem best to its own assembly or Convention." After all, Franklin's union was a second choice to restoration of the imperial community. It only became "perpetual" if that first preference failed. By contrast, the "perpetual" union approved by Congress in November 1777 excluded any reference to Britain at all and its federal core was laid out more emphatically: "Each state retains its sovereignty, freedom and independence, and every power, jurisdiction and right, which is not by this confederation expressly delegated to the United States, in Congress assembled."

Over the years much—perhaps too much—has been made of the limited authority that Congress, as the national government, could exercise in this new confederation. It would remain, as it had been from the beginning, a unicameral assembly where delegates voted by state rather than as individuals. Although there would be departments organized to perform specialized functions—most notably war, foreign affairs, and finance—they would be run by members of Congress, with a handful of staff to assist them. There was no separate executive; there was no national judiciary. All votes on matters of any legislative significance required a two-thirds majority to carry. Any proposal to amend the Articles, once they had been ratified by all of the states, would require that same unanimity. Congress had no authority to tax individuals or the states directly, nor could it regulate commerce. It issued bonds, printed paper money, and solicited loans but, having no independent source of income, it depended on a state requisition system. Whether for general funds or paying for the tools of war or putting armies in the field or sending ships to sea, Congress would set a budget and then depend on the states to pay their share by their own methods.

Emulating states that set term limits in their own governments, Congress was concerned that no one with a seat in it become too comfortable. No delegate chosen as the president of Congress could serve in that position more than once every three years. All delegates were prohibited from serving for any more than three years, and two consecutively, in a range of six. The states would have to provide for them because Congress would not pay its members salaries.

Thus, some might now ask, were the men serving in Congress real representatives or mere delegates, with Congress itself more of a consultative committee than a true legislative body? It did have the sole authority to declare war, though states had the right of self-defense. It had the sole right to negotiate treaties with foreign nations, though individual states could, with Congress's permission, discuss matters of mutual concern with other countries. Congress, not the states, would handle Indian affairs. States could coin their own money but Congress would regulate exchange rates and provide for uniform weights and measures.

Of greater import when it came to defining the nature of the union, the "free citizens" of all the states were to enjoy the equal protection of the law throughout the union. Moreover, in any dispute pitting one state against another, if Congress acted as the mediator, its findings would be binding on the contending parties. And all of this, as the articles stated at the beginning and reaffirmed at the end, would occur within a "perpetual union," its terms to be "inviolably observed" by every state that was part of it—which would seem to be saying that this was more than a mere "league of friendship."

That Congress remained the sole constitutionally defined organ of national government under the articles was only in part a reaction to fears of an overly powerful executive, fears deepened in the crisis leading to war that had pitted representative assemblies against royally appointed governors in most of the rebellious colonies. Future revolutionaries had also read in John Locke that the legislature should be the most powerful branch of government because only it represented the people, and all political legitimacy flowed from and through them. If they knew their John Locke, they may also have known their David Hume, who reminded readers that all governments, no matter their form, depend for their survival on the consent of the governed. Loyalists had never accepted the revolutionaries' claim of rightful rule. The great test would now be if the revolutionaries could agree among themselves on how to form their federal republic.

States and nation had been created in the midst of war. In that desperate setting, members of the national congress were less likely to discuss fundamentals when forming a government than their counterparts in the states. Governmental formation on the state level produced some of the more intense political debates in the new nation, as old principles were reaffirmed within a new context. "All government of right originates from the people, is founded by compact only, and instituted solely for the good of the whole," proclaimed Maryland's 1776 constitution. Other states included similar pronouncements, as constitution-making underscored that they were exercising the most fundamental power in politics. Virtually all affirmed that men's rights were antecedent to government, that government may recognize those rights but it did not create them, that the people were the source of all legitimate authority and the protection of their rights was the first obligation of any government. The people had the right to be heard, indirectly through their representatives or directly, if necessary, including taking back whatever authority they had delegated to government. John Adams's ideal of "a government of laws, and not of men" was hardly peculiar to Massachusetts, which included that phrase in its constitution.

Pennsylvania is often singled out as the state that most self-consciously democratized itself as it became part of a new federal union. Under its first state constitution, it eliminated the office of governor in favor of an executive council chosen by the assembly. It adjusted its single house assembly to make it more answerable to the people. Elections were annual, the number of years a member could serve or run for office was regulated, debates were open to the public, and proceedings were to be reported in the press each week so that the people would know what their representatives were doing.

Not surprisingly, some voters expected representatives to do as they were instructed—because there could be no legitimate vote of conscience if it went against constituent preferences. Actual representation would thereby purge government of any vestigial virtual representation. Specific property requirements were all but eliminated for those otherwise qualified to vote. Those who could vote in state elections were deemed worthy to hold virtually any state office. "All elections ought to be free" to those with a stake in society, declared this constitution, its unabashedly populist tone setting it apart from others.

Massachusetts marked a departure from what had become the norm when in 1780 it adopted a constitution written at a convention called just for that purpose. Its work was endorsed by popular referendum, the task of creating fundamental law being deemed too essential to leave to the convention delegates alone. That convention had been called because the first proposed constitution, written by the state legislature, had been submitted to the "people"—meaning free white adult males—in their town meetings for ratification in 1778. A solid majority had rejected it. Some of those towns did not simply reject what they were sent; they responded with recommendations for redistributing seats in the proposed legislature and for easing property qualifications to vote or hold office. Some also called for a declaration of rights that would guarantee basic freedoms. That declaration became the preamble of the 1780 text—as a similar pronouncement had become part of Virginia's constitution in 1776. Indeed, popular constituent power elsewhere, as in Massachusetts, had begun to move beyond more traditional bounds and with more explicit assertions of right.

What became the revolutionary movement had undeniably brought with it a political leavening. Nonetheless it did so within the confines of the already existing political culture. It was no coincidence that as colonists previously on the fringe of public life became more directly involved with the political agitation producing committees of correspondence and provincial conventions, and then took up arms to defend what were being claimed as American rights, that restrictions would be eased. But those eased restrictions were for free white males twenty-one and older, whose property requirements in either land or other assets might be lowered for voting or for holding office. Free blacks and mulattoes, Indians, and women almost everywhere continued to be excluded from political participation, in some places by formal restrictions, in others by informal social practices; likewise for religious exclusions that affected Catholics and non-Christians.

Whatever discontent members of excluded groups may have felt at being denied access to power, it did not match the frustrations of some who were already politically empowered. Those frustrations spilled over in what is now remembered as Shays's Rebellion, erupting in the summer of 1786 and carrying all the way into the winter of 1787. Massachusetts was the focal point but the unrest extended into other parts of New England. It has been characterized as being caused by various smoldering differences: subsistence farmers versus commercial growers, debtors versus creditors, hard money fiscal conservatives versus paper money inflationists, politically under-represented west versus eastern elites, even as a contest between tradition and change.

In any event, small farmers and shop owners in western Massachusetts mobilized themselves as if it were the 1760s, with Boston now playing the role of London, and the state legislature filling in as parliament which, in assuming the role of distant tyrant, had obligingly raised taxes after the war. Those feeling oppressed held meetings, passed resolutions, engaged in protest, and prevented courts from taking action to foreclose on delinquent mortgages, mortgages that had to be paid in specie. Springfield, site of a U.S. armory, became the most famous flashpoint. There militia called out by the state government clashed with other militiamen claiming to act in the name of the people. Only a few died and even Daniel Shays, a veteran Continental Army officer who had emerged as the leader of the rebels, was pardoned the next year after he fled into the Vermont country for sanctuary. Lacking funds and not sure how to mobilize only those militia companies it considered reliable, the Massachusetts government allowed a few power-ful men aligned with Governor James Bowdoin to take the lead in putting down the uprising. The unrest that had spread to neighboring states ended at roughly the same moment, with Rhode Island acting to placate its protes-tors while Connecticut and New Hampshire intimidated them with arrests and threatened prosecutions.

The eruption of civil unrest on such a scale proved unnerving to many already worried about national and state affairs. Massachusetts had not had anything to match the Regulator movement in the Carolinas before the war, which had exposed regional and class antagonisms there. Having chosen to govern itself under what some observers considered the best-balanced constitution in all of the states, Massachusetts's brush with anarchy struck many as a dangerous warning.

Thomas Jefferson's reaction to the unrest in New England—"that a little rebellion now and then is a good thing," causing a cleansing in the political realm like storms produced in the natural world—was hardly representa-tive. John Adams, who, like Jefferson, was in Europe at the time, was far less enthusiastic about events in his home state. He was not as worried as Franklin became, and Washington's concern far outstripped Franklin's. In corresponding with the like-minded, Washington returned to themes he had emphasized before retiring to Mount Vernon. The war had trans-formed Washington's sense of nationalism. He once called Virginia "my country"; no more. But he feared that too many of his fellow Americans still thought in those terms and that government under the Articles of Confederation kept them from expanding their sense of community—this, despite his seeing that not every problem coming before the nation or the states was proving insoluble. He had offered his home as the site for successful deliberations between Virginia and Maryland in 1785. There leading men worked out an agreement over disputed boundaries and commercial rights on the Potomac River, which their respective legislatures subsequently endorsed. But in Washington's view—and in most historical accounts ever since—the so-called Mount Vernon conference was proof that the Confederation was badly flawed because states had had to resolve a dispute that he and others thought should be more properly handled on the national level.

One of those others was Alexander Hamilton, once Washington's aide during the war, now a rising star in New York politics. Hamilton represented his state at a gathering now remembered as the Annapolis Convention in September 1786. Twelve delegates from five states met to discuss the trade barriers that had been erected against each other. James Madison, one of the Virginians, had advocated the meeting, based in part on hopes raised at Mount Vernon. He wanted broader questions of interstate commerce to be addressed, with the states working out for themselves accommodations beyond the purview of the national government.

As it turned out, delegates from five states were eight states too few for deciding anything that applied to all thirteen. In the aftermath, Hamilton led the way in urging Congress to call for a more general convention to review the Articles of Confederation and fix its flaws. The failure at Annapolis, resolved the delegates (which included John Dickinson as well as Hamilton and Madison) before they left, was proof that certain problems were systemic, resulting from a confused notion of confederation. This special convention would not simply review particular grants of congressional authority or the withholding of them; it would necessarily deal with issues revolving around the nature of their federal republic and, ideally, better define the relationship between nation and states, and the people in them.

Hamilton had been complaining that "the confederation itself is defective, and requires to be altered" even before the victory at Yorktown. He dismissed it as "neither fit for war, nor peace." Changes that he and others had wanted Congress to embrace so that national affairs could be handled more smoothly seemed always to fail—hence the fate of a proposed national bank and a tariff to free Congress of its dependence on requisitions. Achieving a two-thirds majority for votes in Congress could be difficult; achieving a unanimous agreement by the state legislatures to amend the Articles proved impossible.

Treating Washington and Madison, or Hamilton and Dickinson, as co-conspirators who connived and plotted against confederation under the articles until they could replace them does nothing to recapture the state of mind at that moment. Instead, it would be better to think of them as passing through the same transformation that had carried them from protest to revolt to revolution. At some point they gave up on the Articles of Confederation, as they had earlier on the British empire. For some it came sooner than others. But for all of them that meant wanting something different from what the Articles provided. In that choice they understandably conflated failures of the governmental system with failures that had no simple proximate cause.

So just how badly was the Confederation doing? Critics could point to the failure at Annapolis to resolve interstate disputes as proof that it was inadequate for the political task before it. But then defenders of government under the Articles could counter that, if conditions were so desperate, why did delegates from only five states attend, with four states not sending any at all and another four waiting too long to appoint theirs?

Understanding how sensitive his countrymen could be on the subject, Washington avoided becoming publicly involved in the movement that led to the constitutional convention until Congress formally issued the call. Only then would he allow his name to be added to those of other delegates already chosen by the Virginia legislature. And that returns us to the problem of attributing motives, critics having one explanation for his reticence, defenders another. What is not very helpful is the reduction of the Articles' supporters to defenders of the "Spirit of 1776" and advocates of a new constitution in 1787 as counter-revolutionaries. Such generalizations make for good historical drama but poor historical understanding.

A New Constitution

Thomas Jefferson famously referred to the men who gathered at the constitutional convention as "an assembly of demigods." True, he would always make a clearer distinction between the constitution they produced in Philadelphia and constitutionalism—the quest for and commitment to fundamental law—than would his future political ally James Madison. But then Madison's personal investment in that particular expression of the impulse understandably ran deeper than did Jefferson's. Even so, Jefferson intended no irony by the compliment. And he offered it without knowing precisely what Madison and the rest would do once they settled down to business.

Jefferson made the observation in a note to his onetime colleague in Congress, John Adams, who, like Jefferson, was attempting to advance the national interest by diplomatic service abroad. Jefferson may have been living among ostensible allies, with Adams among former enemies, but both found that they were bit players on their respective stages. Neither had ambassadorial status. Jefferson, as minister to the court of Louis XVI, and Adams, as minister to the court of St. James, learned that life at Versailles and London did not revolve around them or their new republic. Frustrations with the United States being regarded by Europeans as a second-tier nation were what had prompted some of the delegates in Philadelphia to go there in the first place.

The fifty-five men who converged on Philadelphia between May and September 1787 for what became a convention to write a new constitution, not simply revise the old, were not representative of the larger American population. They were, however, generally representative of the elite that had dominated American political life before the Revolution began. That elite would continue to do so for some time to come, at least on the national level. To those who point out that only six men signed both the Declaration of Independence in 1776 and the new Constitution in 1787, others could counter that nearly four-fifths of the delegates who attended the constitutional convention had served or were serving in the Continental Congress. Change and continuity, then, are inseparably intertwined here.

At twenty-six, Jonathan Dayton of New Jersey was the youngest delegate; at eighty-one, Benjamin Franklin of Pennsylvania was the oldest. The Revolutionary generation, we need to remember, embraced more than just one American age group. That Dayton rather than Franklin would comment most directly on the role played by self-interest at the convention did not necessarily mean that the youngest delegate was more jaded than the oldest. Rather, all of the delegates understood that whatever they crafted had to be workable in the real world, satisfying the demands of political pragmatists, not the more ethereal wishes of governmental theorists. As South Carolina delegate Pierce Butler advised fairly early on, "we must follow the example of Solon, who gave Athenians not the best Government he could devise, but the best they would receive." As Madison would explain in later defending their handiwork, they tried to combine a respect for the past—their own recent national past as well as what they could learn from antiquity—with a willingness to experiment as they ventured into the future. Should Americans, he asked, allow others "to overrule the suggestions of their own good sense, the knowledge of their own situation, and the lessons of their own experience?" Or as John Dickinson put it most famously during the convention: "Experience must be our only guide, Reason may mislead us."

The labels subsequently applied to supporters of the Constitution as "Federalists" and opponents as "Antifederalists" are no more helpful in explaining who believed what than the wartime labels "whigs" and "tories" are in distinguishing patriots from loyalists. Federalists and Antifederalists shared the same notions about human nature and the need for fundamental law to be expressed in written constitutions. And governmental forms, they all believed, no matter how excellent, could not alone guarantee liberty. "No theoretical checks, no form of government, can render us secure," admonished James Madison, if the people lost all sense of virtue. He wrote that as a defender of what came out of Philadelphia; he was confident that even his opponents shared a similar view.

All of the men who attended the convention were federalists of one stamp or another. So were those supposed "Antifederalists" like Richard Henry Lee and Samuel Adams, who denounced them as "consolidation-ists." That is to say, their political attachment, James Madison's as much as Samuel Adams's, was to an independent *federal* republic, not just a monarchy-free new nation. But they could differ—deeply, passionately—over the precise nature of their union, and they disagreed over the proper way to distribute political power and governmental authority in it. Those differences manifested themselves at the convention itself, then again in the debates afterward over what had been done there. "The controversy must be endless whilst gentlemen differ in the grounds of their arguments," commented delegate William Samuel Johnson of Connecticut, a month into the convention with still nothing basic resolved. Listening to the debates, he deduced that "those on one side" considered "the States as districts of people composing one political Society," with "those on the other consid-ering them as so many political societies." Johnson sided with the latter group.

He feared that they would be unable to accomplish anything if they kept stumbling over the question that he knew had no clear answer: was there a nation first and, only because of it, states, or, did those states come first and, because of them, there then was a nation? No doubt many Revolutionary Americans had expanded their notion of popular sovereignty, legitimate political authority not simply being derived from the people, but now also exercised by them directly or through their representatives. A few had even come to embrace the idea that office holders ought to act as instructed by their constituents. Even so, that had little to do with whether the American people existed as a real or merely rhetorical political whole on the national level, or whether their only real political identity came from their residence in a state.

The solution to the problem, for now, was not to answer that question; rather, it was to make the question seem irrelevant to the task at hand. That task was to devise a government "formed for" the states "in their political capacity as well as for the individuals composing them." In other words, states were one essential element of American political culture and therefore of any national government; the American people, writ large, were the other. The constitution being drafted in 1787, because it called for a more vigorous national government, would oblige Americans to decide how they could live in a single union with a dual political identity. They ought to be nationalistic in some sense, with a strong state attachment as well. Ideally this new constitution would allow them—even require them—to be loyal to both associations, not having to choose one over the other.

Legislatures in twelve of the thirteen states had agreed to send delegations to the Philadelphia gathering. Rhode Island refused to participate—which made unanimity there impossible. Those twelve states that did participate did not have full delegations meeting together at any one time. The New Yorkers went home in protest in June before their New Hampshire counterparts even arrived in July. Alexander Hamilton alone among the New Yorkers returned. Although he joined in debates and helped shape the language of the final text, he could only sign it as an individual acting alone. Like everyone else there he was committed to republican forms. He did not, as some would later allege, push for a return to monarchy. His preference would have been for those in the highest national government posts to serve upon "good behavior," with no fixed terms. Any office holder elected or appointed by that standard who proved guilty of malfeasance could be removed, because Hamilton, no less than Madison, believed that all had to be accountable to the people who put them there.

Delegates at the convention emulated the national congress and voted by state rather than as individuals. Unlike Congress, votes could carry by a simple majority rather than by two-thirds. That decision proved absolutely indispensable because some of the more crucial motions only carried by one vote, in five to four divisions. A split delegation resulted in an abstention. Those splits were quite common; rarely was there a vote where even ten delegations expressed a clear yea or nay.

During the first week of deliberations, the Virginians introduced a plan to "correct and enlarge" the national government. That plan became the basis of discussions throughout the coming months and the new constitution that eventually emerged bore a notable resemblance to that proposal. It claimed to be improving, not replacing, the existing union, even though the governmental apparatus presiding over it would be greatly altered. Much of the proposal had deliberately been left vague. The full convention was expected to fill in the spaces left blank.

The Virginians called for a bigger and more vigorous national government, with a separate executive and judiciary. Congress would be expanded to have two houses rather than just the one provided for under the Articles. Members of the lower house would be elected by the people of the states. Members of that lower house would elect members of the upper house, choosing from nominees submitted by each respective state legislature. Representation in both houses would be proportional. Voting would be by individual in both houses rather than by state delegation, as had been the practice under the Articles.

The details of the executive office—whether it would be composed of one individual or more than one—were not specified; likewise for the number of judges and courts in the new national judiciary. Nor did the Virginians specify how much authority to legislate the new congress would have in contrast to the old. Explicitly, it would have at least as much; implicitly, every delegate at the convention knew it would have to have more to make any difference. But how much more? That was a key question, demanding some sort of answer.

The Virginians gave the new national congress veto power over legislation passed by the states that, in congress's view, contravened the "articles of the union." They also included a council of revision composed of the executive and a "convenient number" of the judiciary to review laws coming out of the national congress as well as state laws. State officials were expected to take an oath to uphold this new national constitution. States failing to do their constitutional duty could be brought to heel by the national government. New states could be created within the existing union. Ratification of the proposed constitution would be in special conventions organized by the state legislatures, with delegates chosen "by the people."

The new constitution that built on the Virginia proposal was concise, specific here, and ambiguous there, as the delegates decided how to trumpet or mute their intentions. Its economy of language is matched by its brevity. Despite dealing with a much more involved national government and more complex relationship between that national government and the states, it is not much longer than the Articles of Confederation that it replaced. Each component part had to be arranged carefully among its seven articles. That it took delegates five hours a day with no breaks, six days a week, coupled with countless informal discussions after hours, and all of that over a total of sixteen weeks, is some indication of the complexities involved.

Many of the details absent in the Virginia Plan were not added until subsequent drafts. Take, for example, the requirements for a new executive. The August 6 draft provided for a single executive, the president, who would serve seven years and could not run for re-election. There was no residency or age requirement. The new draft introduced on September 12 decreased the term of office to four years but allowed for the president to be re-elected, with no fixed term limit. At that same time the delegates added the now familiar age and residency requirements: a minimum of thirty-five years of age, a natural-born citizen or citizen at the time of the proposed constitution's ratification, and fourteen years a U.S. resident. Determining what authority the president should be empowered to wield, even deciding on how to remove him should he abuse his powers, had to be agreed upon as well. Delegates took the same sort of piecemeal approach to virtually everything else under consideration, with some decisions being reconsidered as they revisited this matter and that.

The much-revised text approved in September would explicitly call the new constitution the "supreme law of the land" but by then the council of revision had been eliminated and the national congress no longer had the authority to review state laws. There were various so-called elastic clauses scattered throughout the text, from the assertion that the new national government was designed to "promote the general welfare" to the proposed congress having authority to do everything "necessary and proper" to achieve that end. The Articles of Confederation had elastic clauses—attention to the "general welfare" being required there too—but they had nothing to match the new constitution's preamble. It claimed that the purpose of this new frame of government was to "create a more perfect union" that would "establish justice" among the nation's citizens.

But do note: the new constitution claimed to create a *more perfect* union, not a *new* union. Instituting a new executive, allowing that new executive and congress between them to set up a national judiciary, and the considerably expanded authority of the new two-house congress to tax, to raise an army, to regulate commerce, even to provide for national patent and copyright law, *all* were presented as expansions of power within the existing federal system. The numerous close votes at Philadelphia indicated just how difficult it was for convention members to convince themselves that they had not gone too far in either theoretical or practical terms.

Going into the convention they had understood that there were tendencies to divide along geographical and state-size lines. In just the decade of their national existence, northern and southern states had shown that they could have different priorities. Astute observers understood that future growth would probably add western states as yet a third regional interest group. Large states and small states also sometimes had different priorities, and their differences could be as tied to population totals as geographical size. And yet the document that came out of the convention does not perfectly reflect either of those divisions. As proof we need only point to one vote—that on July 16, the so-called "Great Compromise" settling on representation in the new House and the Senate. It does not fall neatly into either category; explaining the 5-4 split requires more. Likewise, the now infamous three-fifths compromise dealing with slaves and representation in the House of Representatives, along with postponement of any consideration of banning the Atlantic slave trade for twenty years, did not perfectly reflect a north–south division.

Just explaining why three men stayed until the end of the convention and then refused to sign the final text can prove complicated. Two were from Virginia, one from Massachusetts. They each had their own, quite personal, reasons for being opposed. George Washington too had reservations about the new constitution, but in the end he signed it. In a play on the promise of its preamble he wrote privately that he wished what was "being offered had been made more perfect." Nonetheless, he was also convinced that "it is the best that could be obtained at the time." Given the frustrations with government under the Articles of Confederation, "this, or dissolution of the Union awaits our choice."

Ratification Ratified

Opening the preamble of the Constitution with "We the People" was no doubt stylistically appealing to many. What is more, from the perspective of those wanting to underscore the nationalistic element to the federal union, it made a defining statement about the United States absent in the Articles of Confederation. During the struggle over ratification, the preamble would be decried by some champions of federalism under the Articles for that very reason. They contended that it misrepresented the nature of the union, which had been formed by the states, not some amorphous group called "the people."

Divisive ultimates aside, such language had been a practical necessity because not all of the states had delegates participating in the convention. The committee of style that added the phrase touting the people could not also enumerate the thirteen states. Rhode Island never sent any delegates to Philadelphia and the official New York delegation had left months before. More critical still, by its own language this new constitution would only bind those states that subsequently ratified it by special convention. Nine were required to do so before it could go into effect. Thus there was the distinct possibility of having a political union containing states that had not agreed to the national government under which they were joined. Getting all thirteen states to ratify would be perhaps the greatest test the new constitution would have to pass if it were going to work. They did ratify, but it took a year and a half to achieve unanimity. The myriad misgivings that delegates at some conventions may have had notwithstanding, no convention made ratification conditional: acceptance was acceptance, the risk of failure included.

No state legislature protested Congress's endorsement of the convention's call for ratification. Some states acted more quickly than others while Rhode Island essentially spurned the convention and Congress. Three— Pennsylvania, Delaware, and New Jersey—had their special ratification conventions meet before the year was out. The delegates at all three voted in favor of the new constitution, unanimously in Delaware and New Jersey and by a two-thirds majority in Pennsylvania. Georgia followed in the first week of January, also unanimously. That Delaware ratified first, Rhode Island last, by itself shows that the small state versus large state division needs to be qualified. Delaware sanctioned slavery and would continue to do so into the Civil War; Rhode Island had just barely allowed for a gradual emancipation of slaves there. So much for the notion of a clear north–south division, with the question of slavery's future as the primary dividing line. The further expansion of slavery was undeniably a divisive issue. That slavery was being phased out to the north even as it spread more widely to the south did worry some leaders looking ahead, but slavery where it was already protected by law had not yet become a sticking point in national politics.

After the first few states ratified, the process slowed as opposition strengthened. Advocates on both sides understood that many of their contemporaries saw politics as a zero sum game: if one side gained, then the other had to lose. Defenders of the new constitution needed to persuade skeptics that the states were not losing too much—that the nation would not overpower them as the conflict management that defined so much of government assumed a new form. They emphasized that: the Constitution itself could not be adopted or amended without state participation; states could not have their boundaries redrawn or their representation in the Senate altered without their consent; and although the Constitution set out the basic requirements for members of Congress and the president, the states would determine who voted in national elections.

Such arguments did not necessarily prove reassuring. The Massachusetts ratifying convention was the first where the initial vote was opposed to ratification. Others would subsequently do the same. All of them eventually went through the same process as Massachusetts: opposition weakened, votes changed, ratification carried. In Massachusetts, just under twenty delegates changed their votes between January and February 1788—sufficient to carry, 187–168, but also close enough to show that early victories had not guaranteed ultimate success. New Hampshire became the ninth state to ratify, doing so only after the delegates adjourned in February without deciding one way or the other, then reconvened in June with a still close 57–47 vote.

With New Hampshire's approval, the way was now open for a new government under this new constitution to be formed. That did not prevent contentious debates and close votes in both Virginia and New York. The new national government had begun operating before North Carolina and Rhode Island ratified. That new reality seems to have provided the edge in North Carolina. There the first attempt to ratify failed overwhelmingly, opponents outnumbering supporters better than two-to-one. Reconvening after the new Congress began its first session in March 1789 and George Washington took the oath of office as president the next month, the second North Carolina convention ratified in November. Neither state, of course, participated in Washington's election nor did they have representatives sitting in the first session of that first Congress.

Rhode Island took another six months to go along and even then not very enthusiastically. The state legislature had refused to endorse the Constitution when it came out of Philadelphia. So did the majority of voters in a referendum called thereafter—the only referendum held on the new frame of government in any of the states. Ratification came only after delegates from Providence and other coastal towns warned holdouts from inland farming areas that they would place their communities under the protection of the new United States government, acting, in effect, as city states unto themselves. Even then the vote in favor was a wafer-thin 34–32.

George Washington had snubbed Rhode Island in his grand presidential tour of New England the previous fall. He made a special trip there after ratification to congratulate the people on finally accepting the new order and their potential for growth and prosperity in it.

The fractious politics so evident in Rhode Island, reflecting class as well as geographical divisions, were hardly unique to that state. No doubt the battle over the new Constitution exposed various fissures in the new nation, reflecting ideological differences as well as rival interests. Coastal areas with their commercial and mercantile concerns were by and large more supportive of the 1787 Constitution than inland regions where subsistence farming prevailed. But their divisions were not so marked that the nation was in danger of coming apart. As much as those rural Rhode Islanders may have feared a stronger national government that could tax them directly or indirectly through tariffs, with echoes of the navigation system, they decided that their place in the new American nation was not as precarious as it had been in the old British empire.

There was a give and take in the new national order lacking in the old empire, as trade-offs were better balanced and some notion of reciprocity in a real community gained ground. True, under the new Constitution states could no longer print their own money. But soon to be appended to it were amendments that would ultimately be revered as a Bill of Rights and those proposed amendments were circulated among the delegates at the Rhode Island ratifying convention as they weighed their options.

Civil War eighty years later reminds us that the problems of sustaining an independent federal republic had not been solved with the adoption of a new constitution. And yet when the Confederate States of America wrote a constitution for their new nation they followed that of 1787 very closely. They wanted to improve it, not set it aside. States rights were undeniably more clearly asserted and, as most read the text at the time, the national government was more constrained. The Confederate constitution seemed to say that the people of that new nation had no political existence beyond that provided by their home state.

This Confederacy was nonetheless a republic with a "permanent federal government" charged with pursuing "justice" while insuring "domestic tranquility" and "securing the blessings of liberty." All of those phrases from 1861 repeated the original 1787 text, except, interestingly enough, that on the "permanent" federal government. In another echo of the original text the Confederacy's national congress had the right and responsibility to do everything "necessary and proper" in governing constitutionally. Within a year of the outbreak of war that included imposing a military draft. No state attempted to interpose itself between its citizens and the national government to block that decision. Most tellingly, even with the stronger emphasis on state sovereignty within the Confederate federal union, no state had the explicit right to secede from it. On the contrary, the Confederate

Congress had the authority to mobilize the state militias nationwide to suppress insurrections—again, keeping the language of the original text drafted in Philadelphia. Like the Articles of Confederation in 1777 or the Constitution of 1787, the Confederate Constitution of 1861 created a union that was more than a mere "compact of states." One of those unions would last; the other did not.

Chapter 7

Upon the World Stage

Old Wine, New Bottle

Replacing the Articles of Confederation with the Constitution did not change the American approach to dealing with Indian tribes living within the nation's borders. Indeed, American Indian policy echoed that of Britain before 1763, which had been similar to that of the other European colonizing powers. All had made use of the doctrine of discovery. They reinforced that assertion with their notions about the right of conquest and by land claims made good through subsequent settlement. Revolutionary American leaders took it as a given that they had legitimate title to all of the land contained within their national borders. And as legal scholar Robert A. Williams, Jr., emphasized, "a will to empire proceeds most effectively under a rule of law."

In 1823 Chief Justice John Marshall anticipated Professor Williams's point in a crucial but too often overlooked Supreme Court case, *Johnson v. McIntosh*. At stake was title to lands in what, in 1818, had become the state of Illinois. During the colonial period, two groups of British and American investors had bought lands in the Illinois country, one in 1773, the other in 1775. Local tribes had been paid the agreed-upon price but no actual settlement followed. Those lands fell within territory that had been claimed by Britain after its treaty with France in 1763, then by the United States through its treaty with Britain twenty years later. Neither government recognized the 1770s transactions as legal. A later group of American investors purchased those same lands from the U.S. government, after they had passed into the national domain in 1784. The court found in favor of the later claimants, ruling that the earlier group never held valid title.

The court did not question whether the original purchasers had acted in good faith. Nor did it determine that the Indians who sold the land had not themselves really occupied it. The court nevertheless ruled that those tribes did not have the right to transfer title even if they had enjoyed a right of occupancy. Despite having lived upon the land, it was not theirs to sell because Indian tribes, unlike European states, existed outside the law of nations. Even if the claims of European "potentates" under right of discovery might be considered arrogantly presumptuous, the court determined, that was the world Americans had inherited and that was the world they continued to inhabit. As a sovereign nation, the United States—defining sovereignty as the British had defined it—through "discovery" had "an exclusive right" to "extinguish Indian title of occupancy, either by purchase or by conquest." However "pompous," however "extravagant the pretension" that underlay such a claim, it was too late to adopt another way. In effect, Marshall was conceding that the justice under law the new American nation had committed itself to pursuing would be limited in its application, protecting some groups in society more than others.

In 1783 there were well over 100,000 Indians living west of the Appalachians and east of the Mississippi. Whatever the total, they outnumbered whites in the region for at least another decade. Almost none of them had considered themselves subjects of Britain, or of France before then, or of the United States now. Another 20,000 or so Iroquois living in New York felt likewise, despite their shifting arrangements with Britain over the previous century. Whatever the formal treaty language may have stipulated, they viewed themselves as free people, joined by bonds of mutual respect, not simple subordination.

Initially in the War of Independence both the British and the Americans had wanted all of the tribes to remain neutral—on the assumption that neutrality, by denying their enemy aid, would work to their advantage. Thus Congress's attempts to persuade the Iroquois, along with various tribes in the Ohio and Illinois country—Delaware, Shawnee, Wyandot, Ottawa—in the summer and fall of 1775 to sit out the contest, which at that point was still a revolt, not yet a revolution. Those expectations changed as war intensified. But then true neutrality had probably been impossible anyway. Native leaders were astute enough to know that the British, with their emphasis on the fur trade and concessions granted after 1763, had more of a place for them in their empire than did the Americans, with their emphasis on settlement. In their negotiations, some native leaders did press the revolutionaries to explain why they were having such a difficult time defeating soldiers sent from a small island so far away. Few tribes sided with the Americans. The Iroquois confederacy divided, tribe against tribe, even splitting within individual tribes, though most preferred the British if forced to choose—as virtually all were. The natives to the west were more united in their British preference. So were some tribes to the south—Chickasaws, Choctaws, Creeks. With Kentucky as a wedge between them and tribes in the Ohio country, they did not put aside various differences to unite in some sort of pan-Indian confederation against the new United States. Cherokees were somewhat divided. Many Catawbas—the tribe closest to coastal white settlements—actually sided with the revolutionaries.

Once the war ended, to the advantage of the United States over Britain, all of the tribes hoped to secure treaties of their own with the new nation. They could read for themselves that the peace treaty between Britain and the United States said nothing about them. They sent delegations to Congress in Philadelphia, seeking some sort of guarantees. Above all they wanted Congress and the states to postpone the survey and sale of lands to white settlers before Indian claims had been addressed. They were ignored. Several years passed and little had been accomplished to secure native titles or rights in the new American confederation.

By 1786 the U.S. government had made it clear to the Iroquois in New York and various tribes in the Ohio country that their land titles existed at its sufferance. It would determine the boundaries of tribal lands; it would decide which areas were open for white settlement. The national government decided fairly quickly to purchase rather than simply expropriate Indian lands. In part it was a policy born of expedience: the Confederation government did not have the resources, in men or money, to pursue military campaigns against tribes that chose to resist. But in part it may also have been born of a realization that the western movement ought to be more than a thinly disguised land grab, if the nation were to be true to its claims that Americans were somehow more principled than Europeans.

American leaders were not so naive as to think that the Indians themselves would solve the problem by moving north into British Canada or west and south into Spanish territory. Nonetheless some unrealistically believed that Indian removal could be avoided through assimilation, with Indians abandoning their ways for those of white culture. For the better part of a decade, the natives embarrassed attempts to remove them, even after the Constitution replaced the Articles and raising troops for western duty became easier for the national government.

Before then the national military built up during the war had all but disappeared, as the Continental Army and Continental Navy ceased to exist. Rebuilding would take time. Defeat suffered by a mix of regulars and militia under Josiah Harmar in 1790, and an even more disastrous campaign by Arthur St. Clair the next year, showed that the Ohio country would be contested ground for years to come. The treaties that inevitably followed the fighting were more often dictated rather than negotiated, though, in theory, tribes were being addressed as quasi-sovereign nations. That approach by the national government trumped the actions of southern states that still claimed western lands all the way to the Mississippi and negotiated their own arrangements with local tribes. In the meantime Congress had put an expansive western policy for whites into place.

New States in the New Nation

George Washington had been looking west since he was a young man surveying lands in the Shenandoah Valley. With independence he expected the door to the vast American interior, nearly closed by the British in 1763, to now be open. Ratification of the Articles of Confederation had been delayed until 1781 largely because of disputes over those very lands. Only then did Virginia, with claims to territory north and west of the Ohio River, surrender them, thus easing Maryland's fears of perpetual domination by a larger, wealthier neighbor. Washington hoped to profit from land investments in this newly created national domain, administered by Congress. He also invested in a canal company in the hope that the Ohio and Potomac river basins could be linked and the interior thereby opened to trade and settlement. He saw Continental Army veterans as ready-made pioneers, settling and clearing allotments granted them by Congress, generating wealth for themselves and the national economy. They would be joined by other settlers who would purchase parcels from government agents or land companies, not local tribes, and strengthen the financially struggling nation.

Under the Articles of Confederation, Canada had a standing invitation to become a state "with all the advantages of the Union." Though the 1787 Constitution made no like provision for Canada's future admission, dreams that Canada would someday join the American union died hard. Canada aside, the new national government formed under that new constitution followed the guidelines for the admission of other new states as laid out under the Confederation government in two land ordinances. Congress implemented the first in 1785; it approved the second—the more famous Northwest Ordinance—two years later.

Those two Acts supplanted one passed in 1784. Thomas Jefferson, then a member of Congress, had been its primary author. Jefferson wanted to establish a long-range plan of expansion for the entire American West—not just the national domain created by the cession of lands by rival state claimants to the territory north of the Ohio River and east of the Mississippi, but also to lands south of the Ohio and east of the Mississippi, all the way down to the national border separating Georgia from Spanish Florida. Ideally those states would be approximately the same size, to support numerically balanced populations as well. Jefferson envisioned seven to ten future states whose names were reminiscent of those John Cartwright had come up with for the British-American West before the war. Jefferson's draft included a provision that slavery not be legal after 1800 in any of those new states. Jefferson's fellow Virginia delegates opposed him, as did other Southerners. Congress struck it out because it could jeopardize the larger expansionist program. Under it new states were to "forever remain part" of the new union, with republican governmental forms, and they were to be admitted upon an "equal footing" with the original thirteen states.

The 1785 Act provided for the survey and sale of lands, starting with the easternmost areas of the Ohio country just west of the Pennsylvania border. The U.S. government would obtain clear title from Indian tribes first, through purchase or treaty. Surveyors would then lay out townships composed of thirty-six sections of one square mile each. There would not then be a public land giveaway, unlike the very generous provisions that marked the homestead acts of a later generation. Rather, land could be purchased beginning at a dollar per acre, but in a competitive auction, and in allotments of not less than the 640 acres of a full section within a township. Initially, then, investors benefited more directly than did cash-strapped prospective settlers. The U.S. government reserved for itself some lands and a percentage of any wealth generated from the sale of gold, silver, copper or lead mines—a throwback to the arrangements that explorers of Columbus's generation had with European monarchs.

If that provision seems regressive, there was a progressive element as well, reflecting republican aspirations for an enlightened electorate. One section of each township would be set aside, the proceeds from its sale to help fund public education in the new states that would be created from the national domain. In addition, some bounty lands were reserved for Continental Army veterans, just as George Washington had desired. Although bounty lands were intended to provide a new start for old soldiers, they were not designed to level social distinctions. Officers received more than enlisted men: a major general would be awarded 1100 acres, a private 100. The money generated from land sales would not be enough to save the discredited Confederation government. Eventually those sales did provide a source of national revenue, millions more than would be generated from other sources, but not until well after the new Constitution had been ratified.

The 1787 Northwest Ordinance that followed the 1785 Act provided for the transition from territory to statehood. Territories were to pass through three stages. The transition from one stage to another would be determined by population, so censuses proceeded at the same time as lands were surveyed. During the first stage, when the population consisted of fewer than five thousand "free male inhabitants," the territorial government would consist of a congressionally appointed governor, secretary, and three judges. Once there were five thousand, those officials would be joined by a popularly elected one house territorial legislature and a council nominated by the legislature and approved by Congress. The territory could also send a non-voting delegate to attend Congress. Once there was a population of sixty thousand "free inhabitants," a state constitution could be drafted at a special convention and submitted to Congress. If Congress approved, the stage was set for that territory to become a state.

Five states would be carved from the original national domain following these guidelines. Ohio was the first admitted, in 1803; the last, Wisconsin, came in 1848, with Indiana, Illinois, and Michigan falling in between. Over time the detailed requirements would be altered or set aside but the general principles behind the Northwest Ordinance were still being followed when Hawaii became the fiftieth state in 1959.

First and foremost among those principles was the equality of all states within the union. Technically there was no advantage to being first or disadvantage to being last. The obligation of the new states to maintain republican forms of government, like those of the original thirteen states, was inseparable from achieving and maintaining the nation's federal structure. Congress had passed the Northwest Ordinance, in the words of historian Peter S. Onuf, as an "act of faith," as a "vision of a more harmonious union." It was designed to promote an orderly growth in the new nation that the old empire had failed to achieve. Ideally, it would balance interests and satisfy rival demands even as it demonstrated the American ability to contain republicanism and the impulse to pursue self-government within a single nation.

Most of the thirty-seven states that eventually joined with the original thirteen began as territories and those territories were subordinate components of the union. For a time citizens living in those territories became subjects with fewer rights than they enjoyed in states. As Professor Onuf noted, the men who created the American territorial system consciously mimicked British imperial policy. Congress effectively assumed the role once played by the king in creating dependent societies and setting the boundaries of new settlement areas. A governor in a U.S. territory exercised many of the same powers as his predecessor, a royally appointed governor, had in a British colony. He could convene, prorogue or dissolve the legislature; he could veto its legislation. But he was there only temporarily; he left when the territory became a state. And whatever personal freedoms free, white Americans moving west may have surrendered to live in a territory, they eventually regained once the territory became a state.

The general procedural rules followed in the Old Northwest were followed in the Old Southwest as well. In 1789 North Carolina surrendered to the national government its claims to what would become Tennessee seven years later. The failed state of Franklin, formed in what became northeastern Tennessee in 1784, is better considered a premature move rather than the product of a true separatist movement. Georgia held onto the lands encompassing the future Mississippi and Alabama until 1802. Both would become states in the union less than twenty years later.

Virginia held on to its claim to the future state of Kentucky long after it had surrendered its claims to the Ohio country to Congress. It did not, however, impede Kentucky's movement toward statehood. Leading Virginians even encouraged Kentuckians to prepare for it. This is not to say that all went smoothly. There were many Kentuckians frustrated by their subordination to the far-away state capital in Richmond. Some of them advocated complete independence, from the United States, not just Virginia. They sought ties with Spain to the south or even Britain to the north. The notorious separatist schemes of Kentucky-based James Wilkinson, real as they were, remain almost as murky now as they were then.

In a series of county conventions that met from 1784 to 1790, delegates became less rather than more insistent with their demands once they understood that Richmond was not responding to them as London had to colonial grievances in the years leading to war. When they complained they were in the same unenviable position that Virginia had been in in the empire, paying taxes and receiving almost no benefit from them—Indians unchecked, forts unbuilt, roads not cut—they were not met with a harsh response. Just as it was in their interest to form their own state, it was in Virginia's interest to let them go—an example of how principle and practice combined to keep a lid on western issues in the new nation, whereas in the old empire they had blown apart.

Kentuckians adapted Virginia's slavery laws to their own circumstances. Those settlers moving west who chose, instead, to clear land across the Ohio River did not have that option. The Northwest Ordinance forbade the importation of slaves into the original national domain—bringing back the restriction that Jefferson had had to drop from his 1784 plan for the entire trans-Appalachian West. At the same time, the Northwest Ordinance included a fugitive slave provision, making it possible for slave catchers to retrieve escapees anywhere in the region north of the Ohio and east of the Mississippi. That particular provision anticipated the fugitive slave act that Congress would apply to the larger nation in 1793.

The Northwest Ordinance, then, embodied the nation's schizophrenic approach to freedom and slavery. It attempted to restrict slavery's expansion even as it did nothing to undercut slavery where it was already sanctioned by law. The admission of new states would become caught up in future disputes over limiting the growth of the peculiar institution, with one free state being paired with one slave state to retain "Senate parity"—that is, keeping the same number of free and slave states in the union. Parity did not prevent Northern domination of the House of Representatives but it could prevent the passage of legislation inimical to Southern interests by the Senate. Most textbooks save any discussion of the practice of state pairing for the infamous Maine–Missouri dispute in 1820. But glimmers of it could be seen much earlier, with the admission of Kentucky in 1792 coming hard on the heels of statehood for Vermont the year before. In the early national period such pairing helped to head-off potential disputes; by the end of the Jacksonian Era it would have the opposite effect.

Had there been no sense of community, no willingness to compromise, growing pains could have undone the new nation even in more settled areas to the east. From 1777 to 1791, as a republic within a republic, Vermont embodied the potential difficulties of *imperium in imperio*. Delegates from twenty-eight towns along the upper Connecticut River had proclaimed the creation of Vermont in January 1777. They declared the formation of a "free and independent state ... derived from, and founded on the authority of the people only, agreeable to the direction of the honorable American Congress." Unfortunately, Vermont's self-proclaimed existence was not agreeable to Congress, which used a combination of persuasion and threat to get Vermonters back into line.

Portions of the Vermont country had been claimed, at one time or another, by Massachusetts and, more insistently, by New Hampshire and New York. For well over a decade Vermont sent delegates to the Continental Congress; Congress refused to seat them. Some Vermonters courted Britain, hinting that they might return to the empire if they could be guaranteed virtual autonomy within it. Congress had been in no position after the war to use coercion during Shays's rebellion in Massachusetts; likewise for the rumblings in Vermont. Unable to make good on their claims or their threats, Vermont's neighbors eventually backed down and Vermont came into the union as the fourteenth state in March 1791. But for a time the national government of the revolutionary republic had cast itself in the role of counter-revolutionary. Consent and the threat of force had been awkwardly joined—among Vermonters when forming the independent entity that reconciled itself to being but one state in a larger union, and between Vermont, neighboring states and the national government. For the Revolutionary generation, accommodation among the component parts of the republic prevailed. For a later generation, confrontation would prevail instead—not because the basic issues had changed, but because unionist sentiment had weakened and sectional rivalries had intensified.

We must be careful to distinguish between the intentions of the Founding generation and the actions of those who came later. The first Congress passed a judiciary act that erected the framework for a national court system recognizable even now through its provisions for district and appellate courts, with the Supreme Court at the apex. Congress also passed constitutional amendments that would be sent out for ratification by the states. Both actions, we now know, eventually added to the growth of national authority and power. Even so, the Judiciary Act of 1789 had not been intended to extend national supremacy into all aspects of American law. The same is true of the amendments that the states ratified in 1791, now viewed collectively as a Bill of Rights. That the states, like the national government, could be bound by its provisions was not the general understanding until after the Civil War. Under the new Constitution, no less than earlier under the Articles of Confederation, actual working relations between the national and state governments unfolded over time.

Seeking Solvency

Aggravated colonists in the 1760s and early 1770s had attempted to pair political protest with economic pressure. Those who eventually became revolutionaries understood that their political ambitions could only be sustained if they became more competitive in an international marketplace that they had no intention of leaving. Casting aside the British empire, they hoped, would enable them to participate more fully in the broader commercial world. Eventually, they believed, they would play a dominant role there once they were able to tap into their innate advantages over potential rivals: a vast array of natural resources, an ingenious, hard-working people, and home-grown governments that encouraged development rather than stood in the way. But converting belief into accomplishment proved difficult. In 1768 Benjamin Franklin, reading in London about colonial attempts to stimulate new industries, reported disappointedly that the results "are much in the same strain, that there are no manufactures of any consequence."

With each imperial dispute in the years leading to war—over the Stamp Act, the Townshend duties, the Coercive Acts—patriot leaders had called for a boycott of British goods and support for local enterprise. Consumers were encouraged—with the Continental Association in 1774, publicly pressured—to deny themselves "superfluities" from the mother country while at the same time they threw support to local businesses: home production for home consumption became the cry. They should favor locally made coarse cloth over imported fine textiles; if that meant no gloves at funerals, then so be it. If they wanted new furniture but that meant buying the simpler locally made chest instead of a more ornate imported cabinet, that was the price true patriots should be willing to pay. If it meant not buying a new carriage at all, then they should forego that comfort—joining other individual colonists who sacrificed for the greater American good.

Ambitious colonists were trying to expand the range of permissible growth, not overturn a system that was opposed to growth in any form. After all, a flourishing colonial economy had been an imperial objective from the beginning. Visions of a transatlantic British trade network included colonists who both produced and consumed, in a developmental dream that went back to the days of Hakluyt. Controlled growth would in theory benefit all. So, for example, a water-powered flour mill that increased the amount and decreased the cost of Pennsylvania grain that could be turned into flour for sale in Jamaica redounded to the benefit of the larger empire. Thus, for every act of parliament that restricted the transatlantic colonial trade or local economic enterprise in one category there had often been another to stimulate development in others.

But London's attempts to channel growth—allowing it here but not there—brought increased resentment as colonial society matured. Neither parliament nor the Board of Trade had objected to individual colonies offering incentives for improved farming techniques—better land use, new crop strains, improved tools. Colonial legislatures had offered bounties and premiums to stimulate growth, whether it be for hemp to produce linen or the planting of grape vines for wine or a myriad other endeavors. If the colonists were more consistently encouraged to pursue some trades, reformers like Francis Bernard had reasoned, then they might be less inclined to pursue others that could put them in competition with businesses based in Britain. Although Bernard did not advocate simply letting the marketplace decide success and failure, he did think regulation could be kept to a minimum.

Bernard's carrot and stick approach had manifested itself in some sectors of the colonial economy, which changed even as Britain itself changed. Notably, some British textiles on the eve of war had begun to industrialize. That parliament had by then restricted the emigration of skilled workers and sale of textile machinery abroad showed an awareness of the economic and political implications of what could follow technological change. Colonial Americans producing textiles who did not want to be left behind ignored those restrictions. They sought the new machines and skilled craftsmen denied them by law.

The most ambitious of their textile experiments appeared in Pennsylvania just a few months before the fighting erupted at Lexington and Concord. In February 1775 a group of local investors formed the United Company of Philadelphia for Promoting American Manufactures. "There is but one expedient whereby we can save our sinking country, and that is by encouraging American manufactures," proclaimed Dr. Benjamin Rush, one of the founders. The investors planned to combine home spinning and weaving with factory-finish work, that factory to be equipped with the latest machinery imported from Britain and tended by craftsmen lured from Britain as well. To secure operating capital they sold shares in the company, emphasizing that those who bought them were investing in a new American future, not just one business enterprise. The experiment failed in a matter of months, the disruptions brought by war hastening a collapse that may have been unavoidable anyway.

The economic frustrations that had helped turn protestors into rebels were only compounded during the war itself. Revolutionary Americans learned that the growth that had so often brought prosperity in a peacetime economy was inadequate for the demands of war. With independence, leading Americans were determined not to be caught at such a disadvantage again. All of the arguments about economic self-sufficiency that they had begun making in the 1760s they made with an even greater sense of urgency in the 1780s. Capitalizing on economic enterprise as a form of national patriotism, in 1787 the Pennsylvania Society for the Encouragement of Manufactures and the Useful Arts took up where the United Company had left off. Investors pooled resources, sold shares, sought machines and skilled workers from abroad, and tried to generate public support. Benjamin

Franklin, still in London when the United Company had been formed back in 1775, now back home in Philadelphia, enthusiastically supported this reincarnation. Using the building once occupied by the United Company, the directors expanded operations to include spinning and weaving on site. After an initial burst of enthusiasm, the new company, like its predecessor, fell on hard times. The state legislature bought shares to help out but it was not enough. A fire destroyed the factory; the owners could not raise new funds to rebuild it. The company lasted less than two years, having never brought a return on investment.

The society had been formed in Philadelphia just as the constitutional convention was completing its business. It fell apart just as the national government provided for under the new constitution began to operate. In part the expansion of the national government had been in response to the postwar economic downturn, with the hope that experiments like the Pennsylvania Society factory would have a better chance of success. Historian John E. Crowley has suggested that the new system that emerged was designed to protect free trade through government interventionism. States could no longer print their own money or interfere with foreign commerce. The national government had a monopoly on both as it pursued its mercantilistic ends through policies that attempted to secure the national interest by shaping the marketplace. Congress could now tax directly rather than rely on requisitions. Within a year it had passed its first tariff to shield what would someday be called "infant industries." It also considered backing private ventures to stimulate the economy. Imported tea and molasses would once again be taxed, but without the popular backlash seen in the prewar years. Parliament had attempted to control competition by restricting most trade in the empire to British-owned vessels; Congress passed tonnage duties to boost the American shipbuilding industry. If critics could contend that Congress had assumed the intrusive role once played by parliament, champions of interventionism could dismiss the analogy as specious, countering that the new United States formed a political union different from, and more equitable than, the old empire.

The Earl of Sheffield's 1783 *Observations* captured the sentiments of naysayers on both sides of the Atlantic. Writing when parliament was considering a commercial treaty with the new American nation whose independence it was about to recognize, Sheffield predicted disaster—for Americans, not Britons. Once shielded by the navigation system, they would now have to fend for themselves. They would soon learn that Britain did not need them, but that they needed Britain—for what they bought as well as what they sold. "Both as a friend and an enemy America has been burthensome to Great Britain," Sheffield huffed. Given the dispersal of authority and power under the Articles of Confederation, it "will not be an easy matter to bring the American States, to act as a nation." Britain had little to fear from the United States; the United States would be lucky if it survived at all.

American prosperity did ebb and flow in the immediate postwar years, though Sheffield's predictions had been all but forgotten once a new government under the new Constitution took hold. Coastal commerce and trade with the West Indies may have actually increased during the war and continued to expand after the fighting ceased. Even so, it is likely that overall international trade levels in 1790 were no higher than they had been in 1775. If, during the struggle for independence, the demand for munitions had stimulated economic enterprise, the ravages of war and drawing off of the labor supply for military service impeded it. Generally speaking, the war had not altered the general resiliency of the domestic economy. Most free white Americans lived on and survived off the land; they could feed, clothe, and house themselves without imports from abroad. They continued to enjoy a standard of living as high as that of their British cousins, supporting a population that surged from under three million in 1775 to nearly four million by 1790. Most of that growth came from natural increase rather than immigration, though to a growing number of Europeans the United States had become a symbolic poor man's haven, the land of new beginnings— Hakluyt's old English imperial dream, now thoroughly Americanized.

The U.S. government in 1783 had found itself in the same unenviable position as the British government in 1763: burdened with a large national debt and no clear way to keep it from growing. If anything the United States was in an even worse situation, given the limited resources available to the national government under the Articles of Confederation. Even after adoption of the new Constitution, with the national government now finally able to fund itself through tariffs and land sales, annual interest on its debt nearly equaled that of revenue from all sources. As with Britain in 1763, debt management, not debt elimination, drove economic policy. Even though deficit spending continued, investors bought government securities and the private sector of the economy grew. With increased productivity and profitability, public confidence grew apace.

The genius of the Hamiltonian program introduced during Washington's first term as president was the drawing together of already existing elements to better tap into American enterprise and generate new wealth. Even before the fighting ended, Robert Morris, sometimes called the "financier of the Revolution," had been piecing together a program to make Congress more financially secure. His plans for a tariff—the "impost"—failed to carry, but he was able to establish a precursor to the national bank. The Confederation Congress even laid plans for a mint to coin money, using a dollar and decimal-based currency. "Funding and assumption"—that is to say, managing the foreign and domestic debts incurred by the national government (funding) as well as those generated by individual states (assumption) would not actually become policy until introduced by Alexander Hamilton as secretary of the treasury under the new government, but funding had nearly been implemented under the Confederation. Hamilton combined funding and assumption with a new national bank, proposals to support manufactures, and new plans for a national mint. All were part of the same larger vision: use government authority to underwrite private enterprise and build confidence, at home and abroad, in the new nation's ability to sustain itself.

Economic issues did not exist in a political vacuum and there was no escaping the trade-offs that accompanied ambitious public policies. The Hamiltonian program helped stabilize the national economy; it also helped to deepen a partisanship that, before the end of Washington's presidency, had hardened into political parties. True, the Constitution had not provided for those parties, but not because its authors had been so wrongheaded as to think that they could create a faction-free republic. Rather, they had embarked on an uncharted course; their attempt at capturing fundamental law in a written text could only provide so much direction.

Expanding national authority in the marketplace was justified by its defenders as a way of better securing the people's future. Part of securing that future meant pursuing technological change and creating an environment where what would soon be celebrated as "yankee ingenuity" could be pursued. During the Confederation Era, individual states had granted patents to inventors as they saw fit, with no set criteria. Under the Constitution the national government took charge of and standardized patent law. Using, interestingly enough, a parliamentary statute as its model, Congress passed a patent act in 1790 that superseded anything done by the states. Aspiring inventors submitted applications to a board of commissioners for review. Where feasible they accompanied their applications with a working scale model. If successful, they were granted a fourteen-year monopoly and they could sue anyone who infringed on those rights.

Thomas Jefferson, who as secretary of state served as one of the patent commissioners, gushed that the new law gave "a spring to invention beyond my conception." Not every inventor was pleased with the new system, which would be revamped within a few years. Nonetheless the idea that invention had a social utility that ought to be protected by law, and that only law covering the nation uniformly would work, remains unchanged. However ingenious Revolutionary Americans may have been, they could do little to capitalize on it beyond their borders until the great powers would deal with them—which for the moment, officially, they all but refused to do.

Achieving Legitimacy

Desperate to stay part of the transatlantic marketplace, in April 1776 the Continental Congress had thrown open American ports to any nation, other than Britain, willing to trade. Response was slow, based on whether those potential trading partners thought Americans could prevail, and how badly they wanted to see British power checked. Results did come with time. The commercial treaty reached with France in 1778 was every bit as important as the treaty of alliance. Although no other power formally allied with the United States during the war, the Netherlands recognized American independence and became a trade partner in October 1782; Sweden did the same in April 1783. Merchants in other nations traded with the Revolutionary Americans as well, but did so while hiding behind the veil of neutrality.

Under the peacetime Confederation there were only two more treaties negotiated: one with Prussia, the other with Morocco. Of the two, the treaty with Morocco was the more pressing, not for trade but for security. Morocco, an independent nation, and three other North African states— Algiers, Tripoli, and Tunis, all nominally part of the Ottoman empire— allowed pirates to operate out of their ports. Those pirates routinely seized American ships, cargoes, and crews, holding them for ransom. No longer under the protection of Britain, which had paid annual fees to avoid such treatment, the United States was on its own. The arrangement with Morocco was always uneasy. The United States, reluctant and, during the Confederation Era, unable to pay tribute money, was far more interested in access to other Mediterranean markets than developing a Moroccan connection. Failure to placate the so-called Barbary pirates would lead to the nation's first naval-building program, made possible by the new Constitution, and to an undeclared war, off and on, from 1801 to 1816, first with Tripoli and then Algiers. Leading Americans had never considered ceasing trade to avoid the conflict an option.

Although the United States enjoyed a most favored nation trading status with France, American merchants soon learned that they were far from enjoying free trade with their wartime ally. Contending that trade privileges extended during the war did not automatically carry over into the peace, France closed most of its home ports and some West Indies islands to American traffic. Merchants anticipating that the 1778 trade agreement would bring an end to French mercantilism were disappointed. Those who expected to enjoy expanded markets for wheat flour, cotton cloth, and other goods found themselves closed out instead. In their minds the French violated the spirit of the treaty of "amity" and commerce even if they could not be accused of violating its specific terms.

Plus there were western Americans who suspected that the French had plans to return to the Louisiana country—that signing it over to the Spanish in 1763 to avoid surrendering it to the British only masked lingering Gulf of Mexico ambitions. The Americans in turn frustrated the French. During the Confederation Era, numerous states adopted protectionist policies and the national government seemed incapable of repaying its debts to anyone. Even after adoption of the new Constitution, the national government was slow to reduce its debt and honor its obligations to foreign creditors, its increased powers notwithstanding.

Postwar Franco-American relations proved irritating. Postwar Spanish-American relations were considerably more troubling by comparison. Britain had returned the Floridas to Spain in 1783 as part of a brief, vague treaty. In its treaty negotiated at the same time with a newly independent United States, Britain granted Americans the right of navigation on the Mississippi River—which Britain had secured from Spain in 1763, when it acquired the Floridas—and set the boundary between the Floridas and the United States at the 31st parallel. Spain refused to recognize either the boundary or the right of navigation and, by royal decree, closed the Mississippi to American commerce in 1784. It likewise cut off its West Indies holdings and Spain itself, contending that whatever had been permitted in the late war no longer applied. Georgia, still claiming lands to the banks of the Mississippi, encouraged settlers to press as far west as Natchez and intrigued among the local tribes, trying to draw them away from allegiance to Spain.

Tensions between Spain and the United States heightened. Don Diego de Gardoqui met with John Jay in New York, the new nation's capital, to hammer out a treaty. Jay once again tried to obtain what Spain would not grant during the war, when Jay had acted as American consul in Madrid. In talks that dragged on for nearly two years, from 1785 to 1787, Jay struggled to craft something acceptable to both parties. He could not. He had wanted Congress to be willing to "forbear," without formally surrendering, the right of Mississippi River navigation for thirty years. In exchange Spain would recognize the 31st parallel as the southern U.S. border, grant Americans most favored nation trading rights, and even use its navy to protect American merchantmen from the depredations of the Barbary pirates. The Confederation Congress voted 7–5 (Delaware not in the mix) to support that position as the basis for a treaty, but a two-thirds majority (9–4) was required. The vote had followed sectional lines: northern states in favor, southern opposed.

To leave the matter there, as some surveys do, can be misleading. The underlying division was as much eastern seaboard versus interior as it was north versus south, a reminder that there were at least three, rather than simply two, regional groups in the new nation. Westerners sometimes acted as a people apart, feeling that the trans-Appalachian territory was a land unto itself. Moreover, Westerners themselves could have differing priorities, depending on whether they had settled above or below the Ohio River, or whether they lived in Kentucky or farther south in western Georgia. Americans who feared—or embraced—disunion envisioned four or even five individual republics, so very much alike and yet essentially hostile toward each other. Undeniably, throughout the first decade after the war there were groups scattered around the country calling for dismemberment, for a republic that embraced only this portion or that of the larger nation. Adoption of the Constitution did not eliminate disunionist sentiments.

Irritating as Franco-American relations had become, troubling as the new nation's difficulties with Spain had remained, Anglo-American relations were the most frustrating of all. Neither side honored all of the terms in the

1783 treaty. The Confederation government was supposed to see to it that pre-war debts owed to British merchants were repaid and that Loyalists who had property confiscated could take their cases to court. Those Loyalists whose slaves had escaped and found sanctuary among the British were to be compensated. State governments by and large would not assist in either cause, and the national government could—or would—do nothing to pressure them. Whitehall and Westminster had promised to remove their troops from American soil and were supposed to assist those whose slaves had fled to the British side. In retaliation they did neither. Even if Americans had not provided them with an excuse not to surrender the Ohio country, they would have been slow to leave because the fur trade there, and to the west, was still profitable. Moreover, the commercial agreement that had been proposed to formalize trade relations failed to pass parliament. John Adams would spend a frustrating three years, 1785–1788, in London trying to negotiate a commercial treaty. He could not and returned home in embarrassed frustration, taking his post the next year as vice-president in the new national government.

Officially, then, postwar Anglo-American relations remained undefined and issues raised during the conflict were left unresolved. Not surprisingly, unofficially, relations were often much friendlier, marked by the restoration of many trade ties. British merchants allowed American merchants to buy on credit. The British government winked at trade in commodities like tobacco that no one really wanted to discourage. American trade with the British West Indies, in theory only carried in British ships, went on illicitly. So did trade between New England merchants and the isolated fishing settlements of Newfoundland. Americans goods even found their way to Quebec and Montreal. The point is, old smuggling habits died hard. Both Adam Smith and Josiah Tucker had emphasized that Americans and Britons were natural trade partners, which political differences often interrupted. Americans were still inclined to buy most of their imports from British vendors. And most American exports were aimed at those same markets—the traditional estimate running at 90% of the total for the former and 70% for the latter.

We need to avoid setting too stark a contrast in Anglo-American relations, as if it was simply a question of rivalry or partnership. Elements of the potential for both could be seen even then. Resentment would eventually trigger a war between the two nations in 1812. No clear partnership developed until a century later. But as historian P. J. Marshall pointed out, it was clear fairly early on that Britain, having reconciled itself to the loss of thirteen American colonies, would not try to retake them by force nor would it engage in plots to bring down the new nation. Furthermore, the British were not especially worried that Americans would attempt to move against any part of Canada. They may not have appreciated how pronounced American ambitions in the far West would soon become, but then they may have seen those ambitions as more problematical for the Spanish than for them.

As it turned out, Britain and Spain nearly came to blows in the 1790 Nootka Sound controversy. Located on the west side of Vancouver Island, Nootka Sound could serve as a good Pacific coast harbor. Captain James Cook had visited there in 1778 and the British government licensed two ships to return in 1789 and found a settlement, primarily as a way station for the China trade. The Spanish got there first and the commandant decided to seize the British interlopers. They and their ships were sent to San Blas, Mexico. Spain asserted title on the basis of prior discovery and actual occupation, learning very quickly that any claim relying on the papal bull of 1493 would fail. In the saber-rattling that followed, Spain called on its ally France to stand by it; France, in the early throes of revolution, demurred. The Russians were also interested in the area but did not become involved. The local natives also avoided taking sides. Britain prepared for war, then Spain eventually backed down and agreed to Britain's terms. Though the Spanish did not have to abandon their outpost, they did concede that the British had as much right to settle the area, fish the local waters, and trade with the natives as they did. The interned British ships and crews were released, compensation was paid, and the crisis passed.

The United States was more than just an interested bystander over the months that the crisis built. Americans on private vessels had witnessed the Spanish action against the British. They were treated as neutral parties, since they made no territorial claim. They had anchored in the Sound for the same basic reason as the British and Spanish. They too wanted a way station for the China trade, where they could resupply and refit. They were also interested in carrying furs or otter pelts from there to Canton or Macao, to exchange them for silk, tea, and porcelain ware.

The Spanish would have preferred that the Americans stay out of the controversy. The British actually invited their involvement. Gouverneur Morris talked with British officials in London and a British negotiator came down from Canada to talk with American leaders, meeting with both Secretary of the Treasury Alexander Hamilton and Secretary of State Thomas Jefferson, who passed along what was said to an anxious President George Washington. The Spanish, worried about what Americans were up to in the Louisiana country, did not want to encourage American pretensions to a West Coast claim. Britain, without conceding a formal title, in effect told the Americans that they accepted U.S. expansion to the Pacific as inevitable. Hamilton wanted to work as closely with the British as possible, even allowing their troops transit across American territory to engage the Spanish along the Gulf or in the Floridas. Jefferson wanted the Americans to act more independently, perhaps pressuring the Spanish to make concessions to U.S. claims in already settled areas of the Mississippi basin as the price of American friendship.

In one sense, all of that became moot when the crisis ended. In another, it was an important indicator of growing American power—evidence that its interests had to be considered by the major powers and that it had a role to play in any dispute contiguous with its borders. At that moment there was, effectively, no American navy, no regular army beyond the few poorly trained and badly equipped troops on frontier duty. But potential adversaries knew that could change if Americans mobilized militarily, as they had to fight for their independence. The Spanish worried about holding New Orleans or Mobile or St. Augustine in the face of American hostility; the British worried that the Americans might decide to drive out their troops still holding posts on American soil by force. They and the Spanish therefore looked for ways to avoid confrontation. These were small things by the standards of what would come later, but of no small import for an ambitious even if insecure nation.

George Washington framed the desired American perspective on 1790 nicely in two state of the union addresses to Congress, as the year opened in January and then closed in December. Washington offered both retrospect and prospect—presidential speech as national compass. He congratulated Congress for what it had already done. Blessed by a "Gracious Providence," the American people enjoyed "concord, peace and plenty" as the United States earned "rising credit and respectability" among the nations of the world. Washington urged Congress to press on, to do even more to promote prosperity and to provide security. Agriculture and manufactures needed to be encouraged, commerce expanded, and the pursuit of knowledge deepened—with a national university being founded to hasten progress in all fields. The West could only be opened if the Indian "banditti" were pacified at the hands of the militia, the nation's citizen soldiers.

Sharing his enthusiasm, the Senate and House affirmed what he had set as the national agenda. In following that format, president and Congress had continued the practices of crown and parliament. Washington's state of the union address was an Americanized version of the monarch's speech from the throne to open a session of parliament. The president speaking to Congress and the king to parliament did not just set a legislative agenda; they reaffirmed national purpose.

Yet another parallel emerges, if the rhetoric of George Washington, American nationalist, is compared with that of Richard Hakluyt, English imperialist; namely, the tendency to conflate confidence in the ability to succeed with actual accomplishment. In 1599 Hakluyt celebrated England as a great ocean-going power that had "excelled all the nations and people of the earth." He wrote that before the East India Company had been incorporated or received its royal charter, before any successful colony had been founded on the North American mainland, indeed, before England had even begun to rival the Portuguese, the Spanish, or the Dutch as masters of overseas empire. No matter, thought Hakluyt; the future would see destiny fulfilled, as a great people came into their own and took their rightful place at the center of the world stage. The course that Hakluyt had marked for the English, Washington had adapted and updated for Americans, as they spread across the continent and sailed the seas beyond: the new nation as new improved empire.

Epilogue

Benjamin Franklin died in 1790, between George Washington's first two addresses to Congress. As president of the Senate and vice-president of the nation, John Adams heard both speeches. He lived until 1826, dying, famously, on July 4, the same day as Thomas Jefferson. Adams had been nearly forty years old before he left New England for the first time, in 1774, to serve his colony as a delegate to the first Continental Congress. When he crossed the Atlantic for the first time four years later, it was to serve his country in France. He spent nearly a decade in Europe all totaled. His time there only reinforced his preference for his nation, his state, his hometown of Braintree. Franklin spent many more years in Europe than did Adams and, by comparison, enjoyed those decades considerably more. But however much he was attracted to Paris's salon society, Philadelphia beckoned and he chose to spend his closing years there. Ultimately the many differences between the two men notwithstanding, they were firmly attached to the country they helped found.

Two of Franklin's most repeated witticisms came from the 1787 constitutional convention. In the first, Franklin, while watching delegates sign the final text, noted that he had often looked at the sun carved into the back of the chair George Washington sat in as he presided over the proceedings there. During the sometimes contentious debates, Franklin added, he had not been able to decide whether that sun "was rising or setting. But now," James Madison recorded him as saying, "I have the happiness to know that is a rising and not a setting Sun." The second clever comment was passed along by James McHenry, another delegate. McHenry remembered a woman asking Franklin, as he left Independence Hall after the convention adjourned, "Well Doctor, what have we got, a republic or a monarchy?" Franklin did not miss a beat: "A republic, replied the Doctor, if you can keep it."

It makes sense that Franklin, acclaimed scientist as well as astute politician, considered the new government created in the Constitution an experiment, an experiment that nonetheless required faith to succeed. Franklin was himself a great believer—not in the traditional religious sense, but in himself and in his new nation as a land of opportunity. Franklin's autobiography would be passed down and read for generations as a peculiarly American story, a tale of luck and pluck—success coming from a combination of hard work and a fortunate break. For many, no doubt, it was a microcosm of the larger American experience: Benjamin Franklin, personification of the American Dream.

Perhaps that helps to explain why Franklin's break with his son William seems less tragic than it might otherwise. Franklin chose the American future, his son the British past. Franklin is still admired for having helped build a new nation. His son is more or less forgotten, the onetime royal governor of New Jersey ending his days exiled in London, a man without a country. Learning that his father was sailing home in 1785 after long diplomatic service in France, William requested that they meet one last time. They had had virtually no contact with each other for nearly a decade. The elder Franklin agreed to his son's request, but made his patriarchal displeasure clear. "There are natural Duties which precede political ones," he chided, "and cannot be extinguish'd by them." They met in Southampton, England, with all of the awkwardness we could imagine. To those who would counter that the elder Franklin too had forgotten his duty by betraying his king, he might have countered that the king had betrayed his trust first by denying him his rightful future. His son, like his king, had taken the wrong side in history, not just in the idealized imperial family. Besides, as grandfather, Benjamin had succeeded: William's son was closer to his grandfather than to his own father. In Benjamin's view, William's wrong choice had been fundamental, even primal. Thus the reminder in the codicil Benjamin added to his will, where he left but a pittance to William. "The part he played against me in the late war," Franklin lectured his son—and shared with posterity, "will account for my leaving him no more of the estate than he endeavored to deprive me of."

By contrast, it was not John Quincy Adams, the son, that made John Adams, the father, uneasy; it was the nation they both dedicated themselves to serving. The father, his own life nearing an end, was no doubt pleased that his son was president of the United States, but he was less pleased with what the country had become. John Quincy, after all, took office under a cloud, accused of being part of a "corrupt bargain" that denied the presidency to Andrew Jackson. The elder Adams, had he lived, would have taken no joy in Jackson's victory four years later, not simply because it kept his son from serving a second term, but because he worried that a nation that elevated Jackson to its highest office had lost its sense of what constituted effective leadership in an increasingly democratic age—for free white males, that is. The so-called "Age of Jackson" embraced Indian removal, did nothing to prevent the spread of slavery or extend political rights to women.

John Adams is, unfairly, often reduced to a weak, spiteful man who worried too much about his personal reputation in life and what later generations would remember about him in death. His concerns actually ran much deeper. "Posterity! You will never know what it cost the Present Generation, to preserve your Freedom!" he sighed. "I hope you will make good Use of it," urged the optimist in him. But if those future Americans did not, grumbled the pessimist, "I shall repent to Heaven, that I ever took half the pains to preserve it." Despite all of the changes that he had witnessed— all of the changes that he had helped make possible, Adams was less sanguine than Franklin that Americans could escape the cycles of history.

Still, he shared his son's satisfaction that the American empire continued to grow with each new decade. As vice-president, his nation had not achieved a formal presence in the Pacific Northwest. As secretary of state under President James Monroe, John Quincy Adams negotiated the 1819 treaty that secured what had been East Florida to the union, gave the United States a claim (shared, for a time, with Britain) to the western edge of the continent, and a clearer title to lands that leading Americans considered part of the Louisiana Purchase sixteen years before. West Florida had already been annexed to the United States; Spain could do little more than lodge a feeble protest. Native peoples did not simply acquiesce in their incorporation and, for many, their eventual removal, but, over time, resistance proved futile. Within just a few years Spain would no longer have any claim to the mainland of North America. The United States, by contrast, was just beginning to feel its strength, driven by a sense of manifest destiny and mission.

As president, the elder Adams had not sought to expand the nation beyond its original bounds if it meant war with Britain or Spain. In retirement, he took pride in his son's—and the nation's—success by treaty. After all, he had envisioned American expansion across the continent as a young man fresh out of college. By experience both Adamses could have told Henry Cabot Lodge that, more often than not, the flag followed commerce rather than vice versa. And they could have added a further qualification: that if pursuing commerce in worldwide markets was a driving force behind overseas expansion, the farming-frontier dreams of settlers explained much of the overland expansion closer to home. Whatever qualms either Adams had about the use of force to acquire new territory, they told themselves that such expansion was, ultimately, for the good of the nation and for all who were fortunate enough to come within its political orbit.

Like his son, John Adams did not oppose political change that he thought could improve social conditions. His career is testament to a belief that rights antedate government, that government is answerable to the people, and that the people have a responsibility as well as the right to govern themselves and to rise in rebellion, if necessary, to end tyranny. Who, exactly, the people were—or could be—was another matter. Adams and his fellow revolutionaries did not fully understand the broader implications of their populist creed, or how deeply their social inconsistencies would cut into the national fabric.

John Adams would not have embraced revolution or involved himself in government-making if he had not thought his actions mattered. But the uncertainty that lay ahead and the impermanence of what he might create gnawed at him. Like Alexis de Tocqueville, who would interview John Quincy Adams after he had been thrust aside by the Jacksonians, John Adams could not accept some of the policies subsequently promoted under the banner of the American Revolution. He fretted about the people's ability to balance liberty and equality, to establish justice under law, and to combine respect for the past with faith in the future, all of that in a nation that stood at the core of an empire of liberty. They were concerns that Adams carried with him throughout his long public life. They were concerns that marked the best men and women of his generation; they are concerns traceable among their heirs still.

Further Reading

I have listed below various studies that I alluded to in the text, or studies that I did not mention but I think are good starting points for further reading. It is meant to be suggestive rather than exhaustive. I restricted myself to studies that explore the same topics that I discussed in the text, and I have included books only—which is not to say that articles and essays in book anthologies are unimportant; I have written a fair number of them myself. Titles in the first group are all "secondary" sources—meaning that they were written long after the developments they analyze and describe. In a second group I then offer a few comments about "primary" sources—contemporaneous accounts—in those same subject categories as a guide to those who want to explore the American Revolutionary Era in greater detail.

Before getting to those groups I will simply note that for those students writing papers, Jack P. Greene and J. R. Pole, eds., *A Companion to the American Revolution* (2000) and Edward G. Gray and Jane Kamensky, eds., *The Oxford Handbook to the American Revolution* (2015) are most useful. Both books are composed of essays on various topics by leading scholars. The books vary in the number of topics covered and the length of essays on each one: more and briefer in the former (ninety, all totaled) than the latter (which has thirty-three). These essays cover a broad range and all of them include recommended readings. The possibilities for student paper topics that could be drawn from them are almost boundless. Many leading British figures are included in the *Oxford Dictionary of National Biography*, 60 vols. (2004), with online additions since original publication. Its transatlantic counterpart is *American National Biography*, 24 vols. (1999), which has also been updated and is available online. Suggested readings, primary and secondary, are included with all of the essays in both sets. Once a topic has been chosen, WorldCat is indispensable for finding sources. The OCLC (Online Computer Library Center) is behind this immense Internet undertaking. At its core is the old Library of Congress National Union Catalog series, one for books (NUC), the other for manuscripts (NUCMC). Its listings include items in manuscript collections as well as print sources and, within the print group, articles as well as books. It is far from complete and even has a hit-or-miss quality, but it is expanding constantly.

That said, here are some of the leading secondary sources for the topics that I discussed in this book.

Stephen Howe's *Empire: A Very Short Introduction* (2002) does well at what the title suggests; Jane Burbank and Frederick Cooper, *Empires in World History* (2010) is more involved. Immanuel Wallerstein's contentions about the emergence of a world economic system are most accessible in *Historical Capitalism* (1983). Richard Koebner's *Empire* (1961), a more traditional account of that eponymous phenomenon, draws heavily on the British experience after discussing Roman antecedents. So does, more briefly, Anthony Pagden, *Peoples and Empires* (2001). Pagden offers a sharper focus on Spain, France, and Britain in *Lords of All the World* (1995). Ralph Davis, *The Rise of the Atlantic Economies* (1973) traces the rise of those powers as well as the Portuguese and Dutch.

Studies about nationalism and the rise of the modern state often have much to say about the imperialist impulse. Stephen Grosby's *Nationalism: A Very Short Introduction* (2005), which is part of the same Oxford University Press series as Howe's book noted above, is most helpful. See too Hans Kohn, *The Idea of Nationalism: A Study in Its Origins and Background* (1944); and Ernest Gellner, *Nations and Nationalism* (1983). It is hard to find any recent book on the subject that does not cite Benedict Anderson, *Imagined Communities: Reflections on the Origin and Spread of Nationalism* (1983).

Books about the British empire fill entire shelves. For excellent overviews see Trevor Lloyd, *Empire: The History of the British Empire* (2001); Niall Ferguson, *Empire: The Rise and Demise of the British World Order and the Lessons for Global Power* (2002); John Darwin, *Unfinished Empire: The Global Expansion of Britain* (2012); and Jeremy Black's *The British Empire: A History and a Debate* (2015). Both Hugh Kearney, *The British Isles: A History of Four Nations* (1989) and Michael Hechter, *Internal Colonialism: The Celtic Fringe in British National Development, 1536–1966* (1975) emphasize how the formation of the United Kingdom involved cultural consolidation and political subjugation. David Armitage, *The Ideological Origins of the British Empire* (2000) takes the tale far beyond home waters. Angus Calder, *Revolutionary Empire: The Rise of the English-Speaking Empires from the Fifteenth Century to the 1780s* (1981); David Scott, *Leviathan: The Rise of Britain as a World Power* (2013) and Eliga Gould, *The Persistence of Empire* (2000) focus more on the time period and the regions that I discuss. See too Anthony McFarlane, *The British in the Americas, 1480–1815* (1994); Stephen J. Hornsby, *British Atlantic, American Frontier* (2005); John K. Thornton's sweeping *A Cultural History of the Atlantic World, 1250–1820* (2012); Anna Suranyi, *The Atlantic Connection: A History of the Atlantic World, 1450–1900* (2015); D. W.

Meinig's pioneering *Atlantic America, 1492–1800* (1986); and Bernard Bailyn, *Atlantic History: Concept and Contours* (2005).

Niall Ferguson carried his interest in the British empire over to the American variation on it in *Colossus: The Price of America's Empire* (2004). Walter A. McDougall, *Promised Land, Crusader State: The American Encounter with the World Since 1776* (1997); Thomas Bender, *A Nation Among Nations: America's Place in World History* (2006); and Charles A. Maier, *Among Empires: American Ascendancy and Its Predecessors* (2006) contemplate the American place in the larger world. William Appleman Williams, leader of the so-called "New Left" historians of American diplomacy, made his most inclusive statement in *Empire as a Way of Life* (1980), continuing what he had begun with *The Tragedy of American Diplomacy* (1959). Richard Van Alstyne, *The Rising American Empire* (1960) is less doctrinaire than Williams.

The persistent problems of American colonies in a British empire are the central concern of Charles M. Andrews's *The Colonial Background of the American Revolution* (revised ed., 1931). Andrews saw a distinction between Britain's approach to empire before 1763 and the policies that came after. So did Oliver M. Dickerson, *The Navigation Acts and the American Revolution* (1951). Thomas C. Barrow, *Trade and Empire: The British Customs Service in America, 1660–1775* (1967) did not. The complicated relationship between American economic growth and British restrictions informs John J. McCusker and Russell R. Menard, *The Economy of British America, 1607–1789* (1985). Lawrence A. Harper, *The English Navigation Laws: A Seventeenth-Century Experiment in Social Engineering* (1939) remains a classic, stressing the need for a larger perspective than just that of British Americans in assessing the system. Michael Kammen, *Empire and Interest: The American Colonies and the Politics of Mercantilism* (1970) contends that Britain's imperial policy in the 1760s–1770s became the creature of special interest groups. John Brewer, *The Sinews of Power: War, Money and the English State, 1688–1783* (1988) connects Britain's imperial rise with national deficit spending. Timothy Breen, *The Marketplace of Revolution: How Consumer Politics Shaped American Independence* (2005) is most suggestive.

Max Savelle, *The Origins of American Diplomacy: The International History of Angloamerica, 1492–1763* (1967) places colonial American history firmly within the context of worldwide European competition. The four wars for empire are reviewed succinctly in Howard W. Peckham, *The Colonial Wars, 1689–1762* (1964); and in more detail by Douglas Edward Leach, *Arms for Empire: A Military History of the British Colonies in North America, 1607–1763* (1973). Fred Anderson's lengthy *Crucible of War: The Seven Years' War and the Fate of Empire in British North America, 1754–1766* (2000) is now the standard account. Also see Daniel Baugh, *The Global Seven Years War, 1754–1763: Britain and France in a*

Great Power Contest (2011). Jeremy Black, *Britain as a Military Power, 1688–1815* (1999) and Bruce Lenman, *Britain's Colonial Wars, 1688–1783* (2001) cover a longer span.

How Native Americans fared in all of this is examined in Daniel K. Richter, *Facing East from Indian Country: A Native History of Early America* (2001). Also see Colin G. Calloways's *The Scratch of a Pen: 1763 and the Transformation of North America* (2006), which is part of a "Pivotal Moments in American History" series published by Oxford. The moral and legal sides to Indian dispossession are examined in L. C. Green and Olive P. Dickason, *The Law of Nations and the New World* (1989); and Ken MacMillan, *Sovereignty and Possession in the English New World* (2006). More generally, Francis Jennings did much to re-orient the study of early American history with *The Invasion of America* (1975) and his exploration of "Indians, Colonialism, and the Cant of Conquest." Jennings tried his hand at Revolutionary Era history with *The Creation of America: Through Revolution to Empire* (2000), keeping the same tone to discuss a different group.

For the period dating from the French and Indian War to the Declaration of Independence, when protest turned to revolt and then to revolution, *Empire or Independence, 1760–1776* (1976) reviews the issues in the form of a dialogue between Ian R. Christie (a British scholar) and Benjamin W. Labaree (an American). Robert C. Tucker and David C. Hendrickson, *The Fall of the First British Empire* (1982) also take a creative approach. British policy over this period is reviewed expertly in a trilogy by Peter D. G. Thomas: *British Politics and the Stamp Act* Crisis (1975); *The Townshend Duties Crisis* (1987); and *Tea Party to Independence* (1991).

Jack P. Greene carefully examines the differing American and British notions of rights in the empire in *Peripheries and Center: Constitutional Development in the Extended Polities of Britain and the United States, 1607–1788* (1986) and urges caution in generalizing about the shaping of a distinctive American way in *Pursuits of Happiness: The Social Development of Early Modern British Colonies and the Formation of American Culture* (1988). Also see Craig Yirush, *Settlers, Liberty, and Empire: The Roots of Early American Political Theory, 1675–1775* (2011); John Phillip Reid's magnum opus, *A Constitutional History of the American Revolution* (1986–1993), which Reid summarized in an abridged version by the same title (1995). Professor Reid added to our understanding of the competition between imperial British and local American power, focusing on Boston, in his *In a Rebellious Spirit* (1979). Also see Bernard Bailyn, *The Ideological Origins of the American Revolution* (1967); and two model case studies: Hiller B. Zobel, *The Boston Massacre* (1970); and Benjamin Woods Labaree, *The Boston Tea Party* (1964).

Jerrilyn Greene Marston, *King and Congress: The Transfer of Political Legitimacy, 1774–1776* (1987); and Jack N. Rakove, *The Beginnings of*

National Politics: An Interpretive History of the Continental Congress (1979) are both fine studies. Pauline Maier's *American Scripture: Making the Declaration of Independence* (1997) puts the text into perspective, the expression of a state of mind that went far beyond Thomas Jefferson or his colleagues in the Continental Congress. Carl Becker's *The Declaration of Independence: A Study in the History of Political Ideas* (1948; orig. ed., 1922) has yet to be displaced. Edward Dumbauld, *The Declaration of Independence and What It Means Today* (1950) breaks the Declaration down into its component parts. David Armitage, *The Declaration of Independence: A Global History* (2007) traces the Declaration's larger impact. Staughton Lynd's *Intellectual Origins of American Radicalism* (1968) captures the frustrations of a historian who wishes that the Declaration would inspire even greater efforts at achieving social justice.

Don Higginbotham's *The War of American Independence: Military Attitudes, Policies, and Practice, 1763–1789* (1971) is unsurpassed as an overview of the conflict. Piers Mackesy's *The War for America, 1775–1783* (1964) complements Higginbotham nicely, with Higginbotham focusing on the American view, and Mackesy the British. John Ferling's *Almost A Victory: The American Victory in the War of Independence* (2007) offers a nice overview. See too Jeremy Black, *War for America: The Fight for Independence, 1775–1783* (1991); Stephen Conway's *The War of American Independence, 1775–1783* (1995) and, more broadly, Conway's *The British Isles and the War of American Independence* (2000). William Seymour offers some pointed criticisms of the British approach in *The Price of Folly: British Blunders in the War of American Independence* (1995). Andrew Jackson O'Shaughnessy does so more expansively in *The Men Who Lost America: British Leadership, the American Revolution, and the Fate of Empire* (2014). Leading studies of the war that tout their critical tone include Broadus Mitchell, *The Price of Independence: A Realistic View of the American Revolution* (1974); Norman Gelb, *Less Than Glory: A Revisionist's View of the American Revolution* (1984); and Robert Harvey, *"A Few Bloody Noses": The Realities and Mythologies of the American Revolution* (2001).

There are many fine specialized studies about the war, on both land and sea. For maritime affairs there are, in just a sampling: Barbara W. Tuchman, *The First Salute: A View of the American Revolution* (1988); Nathan W. Miller, *Sea of Glory: A Naval History of the American Revolution* (1974); William M. Fowler, Jr., *Rebels Under Sail: The American Navy during the Revolution* (1976); Robert H. Patton, *Patriot Pirates: The Privateer War for Freedom and Fortune in the American Revolution* (2008); John A. Tilley, *The British Navy and the American Revolution* (1987); and Jonathan R. Dull, *The French Navy and American Independence: A Study of Arms and Diplomacy, 1774–1787* (1975).

On the land side there are various books that go beyond the "bugles and sabers" approach, to set military history into a larger context. In addition to reliable accounts of most major campaigns and decisive battles, too numerous to list here, there are explorations of other war-related topics. Among those that stand out are Michael Stephenson, *Patriot Battles: How the War of Independence Was Fought* (2007); Matthew H. Spring, *With Zeal and Bayonets Only: The British Army on Campaign in North America, 1775–1783* (2008); Mark V. Kwasny, *Washington's Partisan War, 1775–1783* (1996); Sarah J. Purcell, *Sealed With Blood: War, Sacrifice, and Memory in Revolutionary America* (2002); Charles Royster, *A Revolutionary People at War: The Continental Army and American Character, 1775–1783* (1979); James Kirby Martin and Mark Edward Lender, *A Respectable Army: The Military Origins of the Republic, 1763–1789* (1982); E. Wayne Carp, *To Starve the Army at Pleasure: Continental Army Administration and American Political Culture* (1984); John A. Nagy, *Rebellion in the Ranks: Mutinies of the American Revolution* (2008); and Edwin G. Burrows, *Forgotten Patriots: The Untold Story of American Prisoners During the Revolutionary War* (2008). That the war dragged on after Cornwallis's surrender is emphasized in both Thomas Fleming, *The Perils of Peace: America's Struggle for Survival After Yorktown* (2007); and William M. Fowler Jr., *American Crisis: George Washington and the Dangerous Two Years After Yorktown, 1781–1783* (2011).

For the war in a broader international context see Richard Van Alstyne, *Empire and Independence: The International History of the American Revolution* (1965); and R. Ernest Dupuy, Gay Hammerman, and Grace P. Hayes, *The American Revolution: A Global War* (1977). William C. Stinchcombe focused on *The American Revolution and the French Alliance* (1969). Also see Isabel de Madariaga, *Britain, Russia and the Armed Neutrality of 1780* (1962). For the intricate negotiations leading to peace see Jonathan R. Dull's *A Diplomatic History of the American Revolution* (1985); and earlier overtures in Weldon A. Brown, *Empire or Independence: A Study in the Failure of Reconciliation, 1774–1781* (1941). Samuel Flagg Bemis's *The Diplomacy of the American Revolution* (1935), with its emphasis on Benjamin Franklin's genius, is still good reading. Richard P. Morris attempted to balance Bemis with more credit given to John Jay in *The Peacemakers: The Great Powers and American Independence* (1965); James H. Hutson adds his variation in *John Adams and the Diplomacy of the American Revolution* (1980). For the British perspective on what mattered most going into and coming out of the war see H. M. Scott, *British Foreign Policy in the Age of the American Revolution* (1990).

Jackson Turner Main assesses the domestic American scene in *The Sovereign States, 1775–1783* (1973). Merrill Jensen's *The Articles of Confederation* (1940), followed by *The New Nation* (1950) attempted to cast the Confederation Era in a more flattering light, which ought to be contrasted with Benjamin Fletcher Wright, *Consensus and Continuity, 1776–1787* (1958). For the making of the Constitution, Gordon S. Wood's

The Creation of the American Republic, 1776–1787 (1969) still stands apart. Catherine Drinker Bowen's *Miracle at Philadelphia: The Story of the Constitutional Convention, May to September 1787* (1966) may still be the most popular account of the Convention itself. Also see Jack N. Rakove, *Original Meanings: Politics and Ideas in the Making of the Constitution* (1996); Robert A. McGuire, *To Form a More Perfect Union: A New Economic Interpretation of the United States Constitution* (2003); Pauline Maier, *Ratification: The People Debate the Constitution, 1787–1788* (2010); Leonard W. Levy, *Origins of the Bill of Rights* (1999); and Anthony King's retrospective *The Founding Fathers v. the People: Paradoxes of American Democracy* (2012). For the Founders' inadvertent—even if probably unavoidable—creation of political parties go to Richard Hofstadter, *The Idea of a Party System: The Rise of Legitimate Opposition in the United States, 1780–1840* (1969).

For postwar economic developments see John E. Crowley, *The Privileges of Independence: Neomercantilism and the American Revolution* (1993); E. James Ferguson, *The Power of the Purse* (1961); and Cathy D. Matson and Peter S. Onuf, *A Union of Interests: Political and Economic Thought in Revolutionary America* (1990). For national growing pains in general see Peter S. Onuf's *The Origins of the Federal Republic: Jurisdictional Controversies in the United States, 1775–1787* (1983); and with the creation of new states in Onuf's *Statehood and Union: A History of the Northwest Ordinance* (1990). Also see James D. Drake's *The Nation's Nature: How Continental Presumptions Gave Rise to the United States of America* (2011). In *The American Revolution in Indian Country: Crisis and Diversity in Native American Communities* (1995), Colin G. Calloway explains how the War of American Independence did not free Native Americans. Also see Reginald Horsman, *Expansion and American Indian Policy, 1783–1812* (1967); and Dorothy V. Jones, *License for Empire: Colonialism by Treaty in Early America* (1982). William H. Nelson examines the nature of Loyalism in *The American Tory* (1961). Paul H. Smith reviews Britain's failure to mobilize Loyalists effectively in *Loyalists and Redcoats* (1964); and Maja Jasanoff reviews the fate of Loyalists in *Liberty's Exiles: American Loyalists in the Revolutionary World* (2011).

For the American vision of a new age brought by the new nation see Jack P. Greene, *The Intellectual Construction of America: Exceptionalism and Identity from 1492 to 1800* (1993); Peter Onuf and Nicholas Onuf, *Federal Union, Modern World: The Law of Nations in an Age of Revolutions* (1993); and Eliga Gould, *Among the Powers of the Earth: The American Revolution and the Making of a New World Empire* (2012). For American diplomatic difficulties after the War of Independence see P. J. Marshall, *Remaking the British Atlantic: The United States and the British Empire after American Independence* (2012); Charles R. Ritcheson, *Aftermath of Revolution: British Policy Toward the United States, 1783–1795* (1971);

J. Leitch Wright, *Britain and the American Frontier, 1783–1815* (1975); Arthur Preston Whittaker, *The Spanish-American Frontier, 1783–1795* (1927); and James E. Lewis, *The American Union and the Problem of Neighborhood, 1783–1829* (1998). William Ray Manning's *The Nootka Sound Controversy* (1905) remains the standard account of that event, which Francis D. Cogliano updated nicely in a chapter of his *Emperor of Liberty: Thomas Jefferson's Foreign Policy* (2014).

Now, on to essential primary sources for the Revolutionary Era.

For British policies toward the colonies the basic primary sources in print form are William Cobbett, et al., eds., *The Parliamentary History of England to 1803*, 36 vols. (1806–1820); R. C. Simmons and P. D. G. Thomas, eds., *Proceedings and Debates of the British Parliament Respecting America, 1754–1783*, 6 vols. (1982–1987), which does not actually go past 1776 but draws from sources that Cobbett did not; a selection from manuscript sources from Colonial Office papers at Britain's National Archives reproduced in K. G. Davies, *Documents of the American Revolution, 1770–1783*, 21 vols. (1972–1981); Sir John Fortescue, ed., *The Correspondence of King George the Third from 1760 to 1783*, 6 vols. (1927–28); and Danby Pickering, ed., *The Statutes at Large*, 46 vols. (1762–1807), which includes all of the acts of parliament dealing with the American colonies. For parliament in general see the website for The History of Parliament which, like many online sources, is expanding what it includes. Many of the papers of leading British politicians were printed in volumes produced over a century ago by the Historical Manuscripts Commission; others were not but are available in various manuscript collections, some at the British Library, and in collections at smaller repositories outside London indexed in the online catalog "Discovery" produced by the National Archives at Kew, and in the National Archives itself.

For the American side, most states formed in the Revolutionary Era kept records that have long been in print. Notably, Massachusetts's move toward independence is best traceable through the *Journals of the House of Representatives of Massachusetts*, 55 vols. (1919–1990); supplemented with William Lincoln, ed., *The Journals of the Provincial Congress of Massachusetts in 1774 and 1775* (1838); and L. Kinvin Wroth, George H. Nash III, and Joel Meyerson eds., *Province in Rebellion: A Documentary History of the Founding of the Commonwealth of Massachusetts, 1774–1775*, 4 vols. (1975). For the national level see Worthington C. Ford, ed., *The Journals of the Continental Congress, 1774–1789*, 34 vols. (1904–1937); the Papers of the Continental Congress (1959), a microfilm collection filling 204 reels, with a later (1978) 5 volume print index; Paul H. Smith, ed., *Letters of Delegates to Congress, 1774–1789*, 26 vols. (1976–2000); Francis Wharton, ed., *The Revolutionary Diplomatic Correspondence of the United States*, 6 vols. (1889); William Bell Clark, et al., eds., *Naval Documents of the American Revolution*, 12 vols. (1964–), a wide-ranging collection which has only just reached mid-1778; and Barry Alan Shain's thoughtful gathering of documents in *The Declaration of Independence in Historical Context* (2014). For the making of the Constitution see Max Farrand, ed., *The Records of the Federal Convention of 1787*, 4 vols. (1937); and Merrill Jensen, et al., eds., *The Documentary History of the Ratification of the Constitution*, 26 vols. (1976–), which is not yet complete. The Federalist papers are available in dozens of editions. Many scholars still rely on Jacob E. Cooke, ed., *The Federalist* (1961). Most of the compilations listed above, which are in print form, have been digitized and are also available online. The Continental Congress papers, which are original manuscripts, have not been digitized yet. The index to them has. *The Annals of Congress, 1789–1824* are now online, which ought to be paired with the First Federal Congress Project, also online, which has digitized the print version of *The Documentary History of the First Federal Congress*, 20 vols. (1972–). When complete, it will include essential materials connected to the first U.S. Congress, which sat from 1789 to 1791.

The Internet has greatly enhanced the research possibilities for students of Revolutionary America. You need go no further than the papers of John Adams and Benjamin Franklin, now online, to see why. Finding something can be done so quickly in either collection—by a keyword search, through browsing by subject or proper name, or scrolling through the papers chronologically—that it is easy to forget how formidable a task it was for earlier generations to assemble what is now so readily at hand. For both Adams and Franklin—and other leading Revolutionary Americans like George Washington and Thomas Jefferson—the print volume collections are still not complete. These projects, some of them begun over sixty years ago, are unavoidably laborious and time-consuming, and yet still essential, since online digitized collections tend not to be accompanied by the so-called "scholarly apparatus" in the form of detailed explanatory notes. But undeniably, for ease of use, the online sources are unmatched. Compare, for example, Philip Kurland and Ralph Lerner, eds., *The Founders Constitution*, 5 vols. (1987), a model print-style compilation, with the Founders Online, sponsored by the National Archives and available on the Internet. The size of the online files and the speed with which they can be searched are on a different level, unknown a generation ago.

Document collections once difficult to consult because so few copies were printed are making their way onto the Internet. One notable example is the *American Archives*, a nine volume set published from 1837 to 1853, edited by Peter Force, that assembled materials on the American crisis, 1774–1776, housed in repositories all over the country. Made more widely available and text searchable on CD-rom, it is now online. With this compilation and so many others coming online, the possibilities of writing papers for classes using primary sources has grown exponentially. It is amazing to consider that virtually every book published between 1639 and 1800 in what became the United States is available online through the Charles Evans Collection of Early American Imprints, Series I. Originally the Evans series had been done on microcards, then microfiche, both of which required special readers and copiers. Now digitized, the comparative ease of use is almost embarrassing. For Britain, the equivalent can be found in Eighteenth Century Collections Online (ECCO), which picks up and carries through the eighteenth century the collection for the fifteenth to seventeenth centuries available in Early English Books Online (EEBO). Magazines published in the American colonies and the early republic can be found in the online version of the American Periodical Series, which began as a microfilm collection. GenealogyBank has gathered most early American newspapers at its online site. All of these collections were made text searchable when digitized. Unlike the Adams and Franklin papers online, which are free to the public, these other collections may only be available through individual or institutional subscriptions.

The next frontier of scholarly online publishing is in manuscript sources. Developing the tools to read, digitize, and make print sources text searchable, which took decades, was easy by comparison. Assuming that Optical Character Reading (OCR) software achieves that capability, then manuscript collections now being scanned without being digitized will be digitized and rendered text searchable. For those of us who spent our early careers traveling from one archive to another, consulting this manuscript or that and taking notes by hand, using a pencil, in reading rooms open for perhaps six hours a day, five days a week, these changes are almost mind-boggling. Take, for example, a project now underway at the National Archives in Kew, outside London. Adam Matthew Digital is scanning all of the 1450 manuscript volumes of Colonial Office 5—one of the collections that K. G. Davies drew from for his print collection noted above, a deep mine of information on British imperial policy in the American colonies. For now the index has to be done by hand, but the scanned images of the manuscript themselves will be available online to subscribers. Improved indexing will only enhance its usefulness.

What was once accessible only to an academically privileged few is now open to virtually anyone with access to the Internet. But then that puts pressure on a new generation of scholars to be just that much more creative, freed as they are from many of the mundane tasks that once defined historical research. Nonetheless, on the most basic level, nothing has changed: sound research and good writing will always require an inquiring mind, an honest heart, and an ability to communicate.

Index